W9-BSY-522

Riverside Edition

REPRESENTATIVE MEN

BEING VOLUME IV.

OF

EMERSON'S COMPLETE WORKS

REPRESENTATIVE MEN

SEVEN LECTURES

BY

RALPH WALDO EMERSON

New and Revised Edition

BOSTON

HOUGHTON, MIFFLIN AND COMPANY

New York: 11 East Seventeenth Street

The Riverside Press, Cambridge

Endicott College Library

PRIDE'S CROSSING, MASS.

Copyright, 1876,
By RALPH WALDO EMERSON.

Copyright, 1883,
By EDWARD W. EMERSON.

All rights reserved.

PS
.1621
.A1
1883a

The Riverside Press, Cambridge, Mass., U. S. A.
Electrotyped and Printed by H. O. Houghton & Company.

CONTENTS.

USES OF GREAT MEN.

I.

USES OF GREAT MEN.

—◆—

IT is natural to believe in great men. If the companions of our childhood should turn out to be heroes, and their condition regal, it would not surprise us. All mythology opens with demigods, and the circumstance is high and poetic ; that is, their genius is paramount. In the legends of the Gautama, the first men ate the earth and found it deliciously sweet.

Nature seems to exist for the excellent. The world is upheld by the veracity of good men : they make the earth wholesome. They who lived with them found life glad and nutritious. Life is sweet and tolerable only in our belief in such society ; and, actually or ideally, we manage to live with superiors. We call our children and our lands by their names. Their names are wrought into the verbs of language, their works and effigies are in our houses, and every circumstance of the day recalls an anecdote of them.

The search after the great man is the dream of

youth and the most serious occupation of manhood. We travel into foreign parts to find his works, — if possible, to get a glimpse of him. But we are put off with fortune instead. You say, the English are practical; the Germans are hospitable; in Valencia the climate is delicious; and in the hills of the Sacramento there is gold for the gathering. Yes, but I do not travel to find comfortable, rich and hospitable people, or clear sky, or ingots that cost too much. But if there were any magnet that would point to the countries and houses where are the persons who are intrinsically rich and powerful, I would sell all and buy it, and put myself on the road to-day.

The race goes with us on their credit. The knowledge that in the city is a man who invented the railroad, raises the credit of all the citizens. But enormous populations, if they be beggars, are disgusting, like moving cheese, like hills of ants or of fleas, — the more, the worse.

Our religion is the love and cherishing of these patrons. The gods of fable are the shining moments of great men. We run all our vessels into one mould. Our colossal theologies of Judaism, Christism, Buddhism, Mahometism, are the necessary and structural action of the human mind. The student of history is like a man going into a warehouse to buy cloths or carpets. He fancies he has a new article. If he go to the factory, he shall find that his new stuff still repeats the scrolls and rosettes which are found on the interior walls of the pyramids of Thebes. Our theism is the purification of the human mind. Man can paint, or make, or think, nothing but man. He believes that the great material elements had their origin from his thought. And our philosophy finds one essence collected or distributed.

If now we proceed to inquire into the kinds of service we derive from others, let us be warned of the danger of modern studies, and begin low enough. We must not contend against love, or deny the substantial existence of other people. I know not what would happen to us. We have social strengths. Our affection towards others creates a sort of vantage or purchase which nothing will supply. I can do that by another which I cannot do alone. I can say to you what I cannot first say to myself. Other men are lenses through which we read our own minds. Each man seeks those of different quality from his own, and such as are good of their kind; that is, he seeks other men, and the *otherest*. The stronger the nature, the more it is reactive. Let us have the quality pure. A little genius let us leave alone. A main difference betwixt men is, whether they attend their

own affair or not. Man is that noble endogenous
plant which grows, like the palm, from within outward. His own affair, though impossible to others,
he can open with celerity and in sport. It is easy
to sugar to be sweet and to nitre to be salt. We
take a great deal of pains to waylay and entrap
that which of itself will fall into our hands. I
count him a great man who inhabits a higher
sphere of thought, into which other men rise with
labor and difficulty; he has but to open his eyes to
see things in a true light and in large relations,
whilst they must make painful corrections and
keep a vigilant eye on many sources of error. His
service to us is of like sort. It costs a beautiful
person no exertion to paint her image on our eyes;
yet how splendid is that benefit! It costs no more
for a wise soul to convey his quality to other men.
And every one can do his best thing easiest. "*Peu
de moyens, beaucoup d'effét.*" He is great who
is what he is from nature, and who never reminds
us of others.

But he must be related to us, and our life receive
from him some promise of explanation. I cannot
tell what I would know; but I have observed there
are persons who, in their character and actions, answer questions which I have not skill to put. One
man answers some question which none of his contemporaries put, and is isolated. The past and

passing religions and philosophies answer some
other question. Certain men affect us as rich possibilities, but helpless to themselves and to their
times, — the sport perhaps of some instinct that
rules in the air; — they do not speak to our want.
But the great are near; we know them at sight.
They satisfy expectation and fall into place. What
is good is effective, generative; makes for itself
room, food and allies. A sound apple produces
seed, — a hybrid does not. Is a man in his place,
he is constructive, fertile, magnetic, inundating armies with his purpose, which is thus executed.
The river makes its own shores, and each legitimate idea makes its own channels and welcome, —
harvests for food, institutions for expression, weap-
ons to fight with and disciples to explain it. The
true artist has the planet for his pedestal; the ad-
venturer, after years of strife, has nothing broader
than his own shoes.

Our common discourse respects two kinds of
use or service from superior men. Direct giving
is agreeable to the early belief of men; direct
giving of material or metaphysical aid, as of health,
eternal youth, fine senses, arts of healing, magical
power and prophecy. The boy believes there is
a teacher who can sell him wisdom. Churches
believe in imputed merit. But, in strictness, we
are not much cognizant of direct serving. Man is .

endogenous, and education is his unfolding. The
aid we have from others is mechanical compared
with the discoveries of nature in us. What is thus
learned is delightful in the doing, and the effect
remains. Right ethics are central and go from the
soul outward. Gift is contrary to the law of the
universe. Serving others is serving us. I must
absolve me to myself. 'Mind thy affair,' says the
spirit : — 'coxcomb, would you meddle with the
skies, or with other people?' Indirect service is
left. Men have a pictorial or representative quality,
and serve us in the intellect. Behmen and Swedenborg saw that things were representative. Men
are also representative; first, of things, and secondly, of ideas.

As plants convert the minerals into food for
animals, so each man converts some raw material
in nature to human use. The inventors of fire,
electricity, magnetism, iron, lead, glass, linen, silk,
cotton ; the makers of tools ; the inventor of deci-
mal notation ; the geometer ; the engineer ; the
musician, — severally make an easy way for all,
through unknown and impossible confusions. Each
man is by secret liking connected with some district
of nature, whose agent and interpreter he is ; as
Linnæus, of plants ; Huber, of bees ; Fries, of
lichens ; Van Mons, of pears ; Dalton, of atomic
forms ; Euclid, of lines ; Newton, of fluxions.

A man is a centre for nature, running out threads of relation through every thing, fluid and solid, material and elemental. The earth rolls; every clod and stone comes to the meridian: so every organ, function, acid, crystal, grain of dust, has its relation to the brain. It waits long, but its turn comes. Each plant has its parasite, and each created thing its lover and poet. Justice has already been done to steam, to iron, to wood, to coal, to loadstone, to iodine, to corn and cotton; but how few materials are yet used by our arts! The mass of creatures and of qualities are still hid and expectant. It would seem as if each waited, like the enchanted princess in fairy tales, for a destined human deliverer. Each must be disenchanted and walk forth to the day in human shape. In the history of discovery, the ripe and latent truth seems to have fashioned a brain for itself. A magnet must be made man in some Gilbert, or Swedenborg, or Oersted, before the general mind can come to entertain its powers.

If we limit ourselves to the first advantages, a sober grace adheres to the mineral and botanic kingdoms, which, in the highest moments, comes up as the charm of nature, — the glitter of the spar, the sureness of affinity, the veracity of angles. Light and darkness, heat and cold, hunger and food, sweet and sour, solid, liquid and gas, circle us round in a wreath of pleasures, and, by their agreeable quarrel, beguile the day of life. The eye repeats every day the first eulogy on things, — " He saw that they were good." We know where to find them ; and these performers are relished all the more, after a little experience of the pretending races. We are entitled also to higher advantages. Something is wanting to science until it has been humanized. The table of logarithms is one thing, and its vital play in botany, music, optics and architecture, another. There are advancements to numbers, anatomy, architecture, astronomy, little suspected at first, when, by union with intellect and will, they ascend into the life and reappear in conversation, character and politics.

But this comes later. We speak now only of our acquaintance with them in their own sphere and the way in which they seem to fascinate and draw to them some genius who occupies himself with one thing, all his life long. The possibility of interpretation lies in the identity of the observer with the observed. Each material thing has its celestial side ; has its translation, through humanity, into the spiritual and necessary sphere where it plays a part as indestructible as any other. And to these, their ends, all things continually ascend. The gases gather to the solid firmament : the chemic lump arrives at the plant, and grows ;

arrives at the quadruped, and walks; arrives at the man, and thinks. But also the constituency determines the vote of the representative. He is not only representative, but participant. Like can only be known by like. The reason why he knows about them is that he is of them; he has just come out of nature, or from being a part of that thing. Animated chlorine knows of chlorine, and incarnate zinc, of zinc. Their quality makes his career; and he can variously publish their virtues, because they compose him. Man, made of the dust of the world, does not forget his origin; and all that is yet inanimate will one day speak and reason. Unpublished nature will have its whole secret told. Shall we say that quartz mountains will pulverize into innumerable Werners, Von Buchs and Beaumonts, and the laboratory of the atmosphere holds in solution I know not what Berzeliuses and Davys?

Thus we sit by the fire and take hold on the poles of the earth. This *quasi* omnipresence supplies the imbecility of our condition. In one of those celestial days when heaven and earth meet and adorn each other, it seems a poverty that we can only spend it once : we wish for a thousand heads, a thousand bodies, that we might celebrate its immense beauty in many ways and places. Is this fancy? Well, in good faith, we are multiplied by our proxies. How easily we adopt their labors!

Every ship that comes to America got its chart from Columbus. Every novel is a debtor to Homer. Every carpenter who shaves with a fore-plane borrows the genius of a forgotten inventor. Life is girt all round with a zodiac of sciences, the contributions of men who have perished to add their point of light to our sky. Engineer, broker, jurist, physician, moralist, theologian, and every man, inasmuch as he has any science, — is a definer and map-maker of the latitudes and longitudes of our condition. These road-makers on every hand enrich us. We must extend the area of life and multiply our relations. We are as much gainers by finding a new property in the old earth as by acquiring a new planet.

We are too passive in the reception of these material or semi-material aids. We must not be sacks and stomachs. To ascend one step, — we are better served through our sympathy. Activity is contagious. Looking where others look, and conversing with the same things, we catch the charm which lured them. Napoleon said, " You must not fight too often with one enemy, or you will teach him all your art of war." Talk much with any man of vigorous mind, and we acquire very fast the habit of looking at things in the same light, and on each occurrence we anticipate his thought.

Men are helpful through the intellect and the

affections. Other help I find a false appearance. If you affect to give me bread and fire, I perceive that I pay for it the full price, and at last it leaves me as it found me, neither better nor worse: but all mental and moral force is a positive good. It goes out from you, whether you will or not, and profits me whom you never thought of. I cannot even hear of personal vigor of any kind, great power of performance, without fresh resolution. We are emulous of all that man can do. Cecil's saying of Sir Walter Raleigh, "I know that he can toil terribly," is an electric touch. So are Clarendon's portraits, — of Hampden, " who was of an industry and vigilance not to be tired out or wearied by the most laborious, and of parts not to be imposed on by the most subtle and sharp, and of a personal courage equal to his best parts ; " — of Falkland, " who was so severe an adorer of truth, that he could as easily have given himself leave to steal, as to dissemble." We cannot read Plutarch without a tingling of the blood ; and I accept the saying of the Chinese Mencius: " A sage is the instructor of a hundred ages. When the manners of Loo are heard of, the stupid become in-telligent, and the wavering, determined."

This is the moral of biography; yet it is hard for departed men to touch the quick like our own companions, whose names may not last as long.

What is he whom I never think of? Whilst in every solitude are those who succor our genius and stimulate us in wonderful manners. There is a power in love to divine another's destiny better than that other can, and, by heroic encouragements, hold him to his task. What has friendship so signal as its sublime attraction to whatever virtue is in us? We will never more think cheaply of ourselves, or of life. We are piqued to some purpose, and the industry of the diggers on the railroad will not again shame us.

Under this head too falls that homage, very pure as I think, which all ranks pay to the hero of the day, from Coriolanus and Gracchus down to Pitt, Lafayette, Wellington, Webster, Lamartine. Hear the shouts in the street! The people cannot see him enough. They delight in a man. Here is a head and a trunk! What a front! what eyes! Atlantean shoulders, and the whole carriage heroic, with equal inward force to guide the great machine! This pleasure of full expression to that which, in their private experience is usually cramped and obstructed, runs also much higher, and is the secret of the reader's joy in literary genius. Nothing is kept back. There is fire enough to fuse the mountain of ore. Shakspeare's principal merit may be conveyed in saying that he of all men best understands the English language, and can say

Endicott College Library

PRIDE'S CROSSING, MASS.

what he will. Yet these unchoked channels and floodgates of expression are only health or fortunate constitution. Shakspeare's name suggests other and purely intellectual benefits.

Senates and sovereigns have no compliment, with their medals, swords and armorial coats, like the addressing to a human being thoughts out of a certain height, and presupposing his intelligence. This honor, which is possible in personal intercourse scarcely twice in a lifetime, genius perpetually pays; contented if now and then in a century the proffer is accepted. The indicators of the values of matter are degraded to a sort of cooks and confectioners, on the appearance of the indicators of ideas. Genius is the naturalist or geographer of the supersensible regions, and draws their map; and, by acquainting us with new fields of activity, cools our affection for the old. These are at once accepted as the reality, of which the world we have conversed with is the show.

We go to the gymnasium and the swimming-school to see the power and beauty of the body; there is the like pleasure and a higher benefit from witnessing intellectual feats of all kinds; as feats of memory, of mathematical combination, great power of abstraction, the transmutings of the imagination, even versatility and concentration, — as these acts expose the invisible organs and members of the mind, which respond, member for member, to the parts of the body. For we thus enter a new gymnasium, and learn to choose men by their truest marks, taught, with Plato, "to choose those who can, without aid from the eyes or any other sense, proceed to truth and to being." Foremost among these activities are the summersaults, spells and resurrections wrought by the imagination. When this wakes, a man seems to multiply ten times or a thousand times his force. It opens the delicious sense of indeterminate size and inspires an audacious mental habit. We are as elastic as the gas of gunpowder, and a sentence in a book, or a word dropped in conversation, sets free our fancy, and instantly our heads are bathed with galaxies, and our feet tread the floor of the Pit. And this benefit is real because we are entitled to these enlargements, and once having passed the bounds shall never again be quite the miserable pedants we were.

The high functions of the intellect are so allied that some imaginative power usually appears in all eminent minds, even in arithmeticians of the first class, but especially in meditative men of an intuitive habit of thought. This class serve us, so that they have the perception of identity and the perception of reaction. The eyes of Plato, Shakspeare, Swedenborg, Goethe, never shut on either of these laws. The perception of these laws is a kind of metre of the mind. Little minds are little through failure to see them.

Even these feasts have their surfeit. Our delight in reason degenerates into idolatry of the herald. Especially when a mind of powerful method has instructed men, we find the examples of oppression. The dominion of Aristotle, the Ptolemaic astronomy, the credit of Luther, of Bacon, of Locke; — in religion the history of hierarchies, of saints, and the sects which have taken the name of each founder, are in point. Alas! every man is such a victim. The imbecility of men is always inviting the impudence of power. It is the delight of vulgar talent to dazzle and to blind the beholder. But true genius seeks to defend us from itself. True genius will not impoverish, but will liberate, and add new senses. If a wise man should appear in our village he would create, in those who conversed with him, a new consciousness of wealth, by opening their eyes to unobserved advantages; he would establish a sense of immovable equality, calm us with assurances that we could not be cheated ; as every one would discern the checks and guaranties of condition. The rich would see their mistakes and poverty, the poor their escapes and their resources.

But nature brings all this about in due time. Rotation is her remedy. The soul is impatient of

masters and eager for change. Housekeepers say
of a domestic who has been valuable, " She had
lived with me long enough." We are tendencies,
or rather, symptoms, and none of us complete. We
touch and go, and sip the foam of many lives. Rotation is the law of nature. When nature removes
a great man, people explore the horizon for a successor; but none comes, and none will. His class
is extinguished with him. In some other and quite
different field the next man will appear; not Jef-
ferson, not Franklin, but now a great salesman,
then a road-contractor, then a student of fishes,
then a buffalo-hunting explorer, or a semi-savage
Western general. Thus we make a stand against
our rougher masters; but against the best there is
a finer remedy. The power which they communicate is not theirs. When we are exalted by ideas,
we do not owe this to Plato, but to the idea, to
which also Plato was debtor.

I must not forget that we have a special debt
to a single class. Life is a scale of degrees.
Between rank and rank of our great men are
wide intervals. Mankind have in all ages attached
themselves to a few persons who either by the
quality of that idea they embodied or by the large-
ness of their reception were entitled to the position of leaders and law-givers. These teach us the
qualities of primary nature, — admit us to the con-

stitution of things. We swim, day by day, on a river of delusions and are effectually amused with houses and towns in the air, of which the men about us are dupes. But life is a sincerity. In lucid intervals we say, 'Let there be an entrance opened for me into realities; I have worn the fool's cap too long.' We will know the meaning of our economies and politics. Give us the cipher, and if persons and things are scores of a celestial music, let us read off the strains. We have been cheated of our reason; yet there have been sane men, who enjoyed a rich and related existence. What they know, they know for us. With each new mind, a new secret of nature transpires; nor can the Bible be closed until the last great man is born. These men correct the delirium of the animal spirits, make us considerate and engage us to new aims and powers. The veneration of mankind selects these for the highest place. Witness the multitude of statues, pictures and memorials which recall their genius in every city, village, house and ship:—

> "Ever their phantoms arise before us,
> Our loftier brothers, but one in blood;
> At bed and table they lord it o'er us
> With looks of beauty and words of good."

How to illustrate the distinctive benefit of ideas, the service rendered by those who introduce moral truths into the general mind?— I am plagued, in all my living, with a perpetual tariff of prices. If I work in my garden and prune an apple-tree, I am well enough entertained, and could continue indefinitely in the like occupation. But it comes to mind that a day is gone, and I have got this precious nothing done. I go to Boston or New York and run up and down on my affairs: they are sped, but so is the day. I am vexed by the recollection of this price I have paid for a trifling advantage. I remember the *peau d'âne* on which whoso sat should have his desire, but a piece of the skin was gone for every wish. I go to a convention of philanthropists. Do what I can, I cannot keep my eyes off the clock. But if there should appear in the company some gentle soul who knows little of persons or parties, of Carolina or Cuba, but who announces a law that disposes these particulars, and so certifies me of the equity which checkmates every false player, bankrupts every self-seeker, and apprises me of my independence on any conditions of country, or time, or human body,— that man liberates me; I forget the clock. I pass out of the sore relation to persons. I am healed of my hurts. I am made immortal by apprehending my possession of incorruptible goods. Here is great competition of rich and poor. We live in a market, where is only so much wheat, or wool, or land; and if I have so much more, every other must have so much less. I seem to have no good without breach of good manners. Nobody is glad in the gladness of another, and our system is one of war, of an injurious superiority. Every child of the Saxon race is educated to wish to be first. It is our system; and a man comes to measure his greatness by the regrets, envies and hatreds of his competitors. But in these new fields there is room: here are no self-esteems, no exclusions.

I admire great men of all classes, those who stand for facts, and for thoughts; I like rough and smooth, "Scourges of God," and "Darlings of the human race." I like the first Cæsar; and Charles V., of Spain; and Charles XII., of Sweden; Richard Plantagenet; and Bonaparte, in France. I applaud a sufficient man, an officer equal to his office; captains, ministers, senators. I like a master standing firm on legs of iron, well-born, rich, handsome, eloquent, loaded with advantages, drawing all men by fascination into tributaries and supporters of his power. Sword and staff, or talents swordlike or staff-like, carry on the work of the world. But I find him greater when he can abolish himself and all heroes, by letting in this element of reason, irrespective of persons, this subtilizer and irresistible upward force, into our thought, destroying in-

dividualism; the power so great that the potentate
is nothing. Then he is a monarch who gives a constitution to his people; a pontiff who preaches the
equality of souls and releases his servants from
their barbarous homages; an emperor who can
spare his empire.

But I intended to specify, with a little minute-
ness, two or three points of service. Nature never
spares the opium or nepenthe, but wherever she
mars her creature with some deformity or defect,
lays her poppies plentifully on the bruise, and the
sufferer goes joyfully through life, ignorant of the
ruin and incapable of seeing it, though all the
world point their finger at it every day. The
worthless and offensive members of society, whose
existence is a social pest, invariably think themselves the most ill-used people alive, and never get
over their astonishment at the ingratitude and
selfishness of their contemporaries. Our globe
discovers its hidden virtues, not only in heroes and
archangels, but in gossips and nurses. Is it not
a rare contrivance that lodged the due inertia in
every creature, the conserving, resisting energy,
the anger at being waked or changed? Altogether
independent of the intellectual force in each is the
pride of opinion, the security that we are right.
Not the feeblest grandame, not a mowing idiot,

but uses what spark of perception and faculty is left, to chuckle and triumph in his or her opinion over the absurdities of all the rest. Difference from me is the measure of absurdity. Not one has a misgiving of being wrong. Was it not a bright thought that made things cohere with this bitumen, fastest of cements? But, in the midst of this chuckle of self-gratulation, some figure goes by which Thersites too can love and admire. This is he that should marshall us the way we were going. There is no end to his aid. Without Plato we should almost lose our faith in the possibility of a reasonable book. We seem to want but one, but we want one. We love to associate with heroic persons, since our receptivity is unlimited; and, with the great, our thoughts and manners easily become great. We are all wise in capacity, though so few in energy. There needs but one wise man in a company and all are wise, so rapid is the contagion.

Great men are thus a collyrium to clear our eyes from egotism and enable us to see other people and their works. But there are vices and follies incident to whole populations and ages. Men resemble their contemporaries even more than their progenitors. It is observed in old couples, or in persons who have been housemates for a course of years, that they grow like, and if they should live long enough we should not be able to know them apart. Nature abhors these complaisances which threaten to melt the world into a lump, and hastens to break up such maudlin agglutinations. The like assimilation goes on between men of one town, of one sect, of one political party; and the ideas of the time are in the air, and infect all who breathe it. Viewed from any high point, this city of New York, yonder city of London, the Western civilization, would seem a bundle of insanities. We keep each other in countenance and exasperate by emulation the frenzy of the time. The shield against the stingings of conscience is the universal practice, or our contemporaries. Again, it is very easy to be as wise and good as your companions. We learn of our contemporaries what they know without effort, and almost through the pores of the skin. We catch it by sympathy, or as a wife arrives at the intellectual and moral elevations of her husband. But we stop where they stop. Very hardly can we take another step. The great, or such as hold of nature and transcend fashions by their fidelity to universal ideas, are saviors from these federal errors, and defend us from our contemporaries. They are the exceptions which we want, where all grows like. A foreign greatness is the antidote for cabalism.

Thus we feed on genius, and refresh ourselves

from too much conversation with our mates, and exult in the depth of nature in that direction in which he leads us. What indemnification is one great man for populations of pigmies! Every mother wishes one son a genius, though all the rest should be mediocre. But a new danger appears in the excess of influence of the great man. His attractions warp us from our place. We have become underlings and intellectual suicides. Ah! yonder in the horizon is our help; — other great men, new qualities, counterweights and checks on each other. We cloy of the honey of each peculiar greatness. Every hero becomes a bore at last. Perhaps Voltaire was not bad-hearted, yet he said of the good Jesus, even, "I pray you, let me never hear that man's name again." They cry up the virtues of George Washington, — "Damn George Washington!" is the poor Jacobin's whole speech and confutation. But it is human nature's indispensable defence. The centripetence augments the centrifugence. We balance one man with his opposite, and the health of the state depends on the see-saw.

There is however a speedy limit to the use of heroes. Every genius is defended from approach by quantities of unavailableness. They are very attractive, and seem at a distance our own: but we are hindered on all sides from approach. The more we are drawn, the more we are repelled.

There is something not solid in the good that is done for us. The best discovery the discoverer makes for himself. It has something unreal for his companion until he too has substantiated it. It seems as if the Deity dressed each soul which he, sends into nature in certain virtues and powers not communicable to other men, and sending it to perform one more turn through the circle of beings, wrote " *Not transferable* " and " *Good for this trip only,*" on these garments of the soul. There is somewhat deceptive about the intercourse of minds. The boundaries are invisible, but they are never crossed. There is such good will to impart, and such good will to receive, that each threatens to become the other; but the law of individuality collects its secret strength: you are you, and I am I, and so we remain.

For nature wishes every thing to remain itself; and whilst every individual strives to grow and exclude and to exclude and grow, to the extremities of the universe, and to impose the law of its being on every other creature, Nature steadily aims to protect each against every other. Each is self-defended. Nothing is more marked than the power by which individuals are guarded from individuals, in a world where every benefactor becomes so easily a malefactor only by continuation of his activity into places where it is not due; where chil-

dren seem so much at the mercy of their foolish
parents, and where almost all men are too social
and interfering. We rightly speak of the guar-
dian angels of children. How superior in their security from infusions of evil persons, from vulgar-
ity and second thought! They shed their own
abundant beauty on the objects they behold.
Therefore they are not at the mercy of such poor
educators as we adults. If we huff and chide them
they soon come not to mind it and get a self-reli-
ance ; and if we indulge them to folly, they learn
the limitation elsewhere.

We need not fear excessive influence. A more
generous trust is permitted. Serve the great.
Stick at no humiliation. Grudge no office thou
canst render. Be the limb of their body, the
breath of their mouth. Compromise thy egotism.
Who cares for that, so thou gain aught wider and
nobler ? Never mind the taunt of Boswellism : the
devotion may easily be greater than the wretched
pride which is guarding its own skirts. Be another: not thyself, but a Platonist ; not a soul, but
a Christian ; not a naturalist, but a Cartesian ; not
a poet, but a Shaksperian. In vain, the wheels of
tendency will not stop, nor will all the forces of inertia, fear, or of love itself hold thee there. On,
and forever onward! The microscope observes a
monad or wheel-insect among the infusories circu-

lating in water. Presently a dot appears on the
animal, which enlarges to a slit, and it becomes
two perfect animals. The ever-proceeding detachment appears not less in all thought and in society.
Children think they cannot live without their parents. But, long before they are aware of it, the
black dot has appeared and the detachment taken
place. Any accident will now reveal to them their
independence.

But *great men :* — the word is injurious. Is
there caste? is there fate? What becomes of the
promise to virtue? The thoughtful youth laments
the superfœtation of nature. 'Generous and handsome,' he says, 'is your hero; but look at yonder
poor Paddy, whose country is his wheelbarrow;
look at his whole nation of Paddies.' Why are
the masses, from the dawn of history down, food
for knives and powder? The idea dignifies a few
leaders, who have sentiment, opinion, love, self-devotion; and they make war and death sacred; —
but what for the wretches whom they hire and
kill? The cheapness of man is every day's tragedy. It is as real a loss that others should be
low as that we should be low; for we must have
society.

Is it a reply to these suggestions to say, Society
is a Pestalozzian school: all are teachers and pu-

pils in turn? We are equally served by receiving
and by imparting. Men who know the same things
are not long the best company for each other.
But bring to each an intelligent person of another
experience, and it is as if you let off water from a
lake by cutting a lower basin. It seems a mechanical advantage, and great benefit it is to each
speaker, as he can now paint out his thought to
himself. We pass very fast, in our personal
moods, from dignity to dependence. And if any
appear never to assume the chair, but always to
stand and serve, it is because we do not see the
company in a sufficiently long period for the whole
rotation of parts to come about. As to what we
call the masses, and common men, — there are no
common men. All men are at last of a size ; and
true art is only possible on the conviction that
every talent has its apotheosis somewhere. Fair
play and an open field and freshest laurels to all
who have won them ! But heaven reserves an
equal scope for every creature. Each is uneasy
until he has produced his private ray unto the con-
cave sphere and beheld his talent also in its last
nobility and exaltation.

The heroes of the hour are relatively great ; of
a faster growth ; or they are such in whom, at the
moment of success, a quality is ripe which is then
in request. Other days will demand other quali-

ties. Some rays escape the common observer, and want a finely adapted eye. Ask the great man if there be none greater. His companions are; and not the less great but the more that society cannot see them. Nature never sends a great man into the planet without confiding the secret to another soul.

One gracious fact emerges from these studies, — that there is true ascension in our love. The reputations of the nineteenth century will one day be quoted to prove its barbarism. The genius of humanity is the real subject whose biography is written in our annals. We must infer much, and supply many chasms in the record. The history of the universe is symptomatic, and life is mnemonical. No man, in all the procession of famous men, is reason or illumination or that essence we were looking for; but is an exhibition, in some quarter, of new possibilities. Could we one day complete the immense figure which these flagrant points compose! The study of many individuals leads us to an elemental region wherein the individual is lost, or wherein all touch by their summits. Thought and feeling that break out there cannot be impounded by any fence of personality. This is the key to the power of the greatest men, — their spirit diffuses itself. A new quality of mind travels by night and by day, in concentric circles from its origin, and publishes itself by unknown methods : the union of all minds appears intimate ; what gets admission to one, cannot be kept out of any other; the smallest acquisition of truth or of energy, in any quarter, is so much good to the commonwealth of souls. If the disparities of talent and position vanish when the individuals are seen in the duration which is necessary to complete the career of each, even more swiftly the seeming injustice disappears when we ascend to the central identity of all the individuals, and know that they are made of the substance which ordaineth and doeth.

The genius of humanity is the right point of view of history. The qualities abide; the men who exhibit them have now more, now less, and pass away ; the qualities remain on another brow. No experience is more familiar. Once you saw phœnixes: they are gone ; the world is not therefore disenchanted. The vessels on which you read sacred emblems turn out to be common pottery ; but the sense of the pictures is sacred, and you may still read them transferred to the walls of the world. For a time our teachers serve us personally, as metres or milestones of progress. Once they were angels of knowledge and their figures touched the sky. Then we drew near, saw their means, culture and limits ; and they yielded their place to other geniuses. Happy, if a few names remain so high that we have not been able to read them nearer, and age and comparison have not robbed them of a ray. But at last we shall cease to look in men for completeness, and shall content ourselves with their social and delegated quality. All that respects the individual is temporary and prospective, like the individual himself, who is ascending out of his limits into a catholic existence. We have never come at the true and best benefit of any genius so long as we believe him an original force. In the moment when he ceases to help us as a cause, he begins to help us more as an effect. Then he appears as an exponent of a vaster mind and will. The opaque self becomes transparent with the light of the First Cause.

Yet, within the limits of human education and agency, we may say great men exist that there may be greater men. The destiny of organized nature is amelioration, and who can tell· its limits? It is for man to tame the chaos; on every side, whilst he lives, to scatter the seeds of science and of song, that climate, corn, animals, men, may be milder, and the germs of love and benefit may be multi, plied.

PLATO; OR, THE PHILOSOPHER.

II.

PLATO; OR, THE PHILOSOPHER.

——◆——

AMONG secular books, Plato only is entitled to
Omar's fanatical compliment to the Koran, when
he said, "Burn the libraries; for their value is in
this book." These sentences contain the culture
of nations; these are the corner-stone of schools;
these are the fountain-head of literatures. A discipline it is in logic, arithmetic, taste, symmetry,
poetry, language, rhetoric, ontology, morals or practical wisdom. There was never such range of speculation. Out of Plato come all things that are
still written and debated among men of thought.
Great havoc makes he among our originalities. We
have reached the mountain from which all these
drift boulders were detached. The Bible of the
learned for twenty-two hundred years, every brisk
young man who says in succession fine things to
each reluctant generation, — Boethius, Rabelais,
Erasmus, Bruno, Locke, Rousseau, Alfieri, Coleridge, — is some reader of Plato, translating into
the vernacular, wittily, his good things. Even the

men of grander proportion suffer some deduction from the misfortune (shall I say?) of coming after this exhausting generalizer. St. Augustine, Copernicus, Newton, Behmen, Swedenborg, Goethe, are likewise his debtors and must say after him. For it is fair to credit the broadest generalizer with all the particulars deducible from his thesis.

Plato is philosophy, and philosophy, Plato, — at once the glory and the shame of mankind, since neither Saxon nor Roman have availed to add any idea to his categories. No wife, no children had he, and the thinkers of all civilized nations are his posterity and are tinged with his mind. How many great men Nature is incessantly sending up out of night, to be *his men*, — Platonists! the Alexandrians, a constellation of genius; the Elizabethans, not less; Sir Thomas More, Henry More, John Hales, John Smith, Lord Bacon, Jeremy Taylor, Ralph Cudworth, Sydenham, Thomas Taylor; Marcilius Ficinus and Picus Mirandola. Calvinism is in his Phædo : Christianity is in it. Mahometanism draws all its philosophy, in its hand-book of morals, the Akhlak - y - Jalaly, from him. Mysticism finds in Plato all its texts. This citizen of a town in Greece is no villager nor patriot. An Englishman reads and says, 'how English!' a German, — 'how Teutonic!' an Italian, — 'how Roman and how Greek!' As they say that Helen

of Argos had that universal beauty that every body
felt related to her, so Plato seems to a reader in
New England an American genius. His broad
humanity transcends all sectional lines.

This range of Plato instructs us what to think of
the vexed question concerning his reputed works,
— what are genuine, what spurious. It is singular that wherever we find a man higher by a whole
head than any of his contemporaries, it is sure to
come into doubt what are his real works. Thus
Homer, Plato, Raffaelle, Shakspeare. For these
men magnetise their contemporaries, so that their
companions can do for them what they can never do
for themselves; and the great man does thus live in
several bodies, and write, or paint or act, by many
hands; and after some time it is not easy to say
what is the authentic work of the master and what
is only of his school.

Plato, too, like every great man, consumed his
own times. What is a great man but one of great
affinities, who takes up into himself all arts, sciences, all knowables, as his food? He can spare
nothing; he can dispose of every thing. What is
not good for virtue, is good for knowledge. Hence
his contemporaries tax him with plagiarism. But
the inventor only knows how to borrow; and society is glad to forget the innumerable laborers
who ministered to this architect, and reserves all

its gratitude for him. When we are praising
Plato, it seems we are praising quotations from
Solon and Sophron and Philolaus. Be it so. Every
book is a quotation; and every house is a quotation
out of all forests and mines and stone quarries; and
every man is a quotation from all his ancestors.
And this grasping inventor puts all nations under
contribution.

Plato absorbed the learning of his times, — Philolaus, Timæus, Heraclitus, Parmenides, and what
else; then his master, Socrates; and finding himself still capable of a larger synthesis, — beyond all
example then or since, — he travelled into Italy,
to gain what Pythagoras had for him; then into
Egypt, and perhaps still farther East, to import the
other element, which Europe wanted, into the European mind. This breadth entitles him to stand as
the representative of philosophy. He says, in the
Republic, "Such a genius as philosophers must of
necessity have, is wont but seldom in all its parts
to meet in one man, but its different parts generally spring up in different persons." Every man
who would do anything well, must come to it from
a higher ground. A philosopher must be more than
a philosopher. Plato is clothed with the powers of
a poet, stands upon the highest place of the poet,
and (though I doubt he wanted the decisive gift of
lyric expression), mainly is not a poet because he
chose to use the poetic gift to an ulterior purpose.

Great geniuses have the shortest biographies. Their cousins can tell you nothing about them. They lived in their writings, and so their house and street life was trivial and commonplace. If you would know their tastes and complexions, the most admiring of their readers most resembles them. Plato especially has no external biography. If he had lover, wife, or children, we hear nothing of them. He ground them all into paint. As a good chimney burns its smoke, so a philosopher converts the value of all his fortunes into his intellectual performances.

He was born 427, A. C., about the time of the death of Pericles; was of patrician connection in his times and city, and is said to have had an early inclination for war, but, in his twentieth year, meeting with Socrates, was easily dissuaded from this pursuit and remained for ten years his scholar, until the death of Socrates. He then went to Megara, accepted the invitations of Dion and of Dionysius to the court of Sicily, and went thither three times, though very capriciously treated. He travelled into Italy; then into Egypt, where he stayed a long time; some say three, — some say thirteen years. It is said he went farther, into Babylonia: this is uncertain. Returning to Athens, he gave lessons in the Academy to those whom his fame drew thither; and died, as we have received it, in the act of writing, at eighty-one years.

But the biography of Plato is interior. We are to account for the supreme elevation of this man in the intellectual history of our race, — how it happens that in proportion to the culture of men they become his scholars; that, as our Jewish Bible has implanted itself in the table-talk and household life of every man and woman in the European and American nations, so the writings of Plato have preoccupied every school of learning, every lover of thought, every church, every poet, — making it impossible to think, on certain levels, except through him. He stands between the truth and every man's mind, and has almost impressed language and the primary forms of thought with his name and seal. I am struck, in reading him, with the extreme modernness of his style and spirit. Here is the germ of that Europe we know so well, in its long history of arts and arms; here are all its traits, already discernible in the mind of Plato, — and in none before him. It has spread itself since into a hundred histories, but has added no new element. This perpetual modernness is the measure of merit in every work of art; since the author of it was not misled by any thing short-lived or local, but abode by real and abiding traits. How Plato came thus to be Europe, and philosophy, and almost literature, is the problem for us to solve.

This could not have happened without a sound, sincere and catholic man, able to honor, at the same time, the ideal, or laws of the mind, and fate, or the order of nature. The first period of a nation, as of an individual, is the period of unconscious strength. Children cry, scream and stamp with fury, unable to express their desires. As soon as they can speak and tell their want and the reason of it, they become gentle. In adult life, whilst the perceptions are obtuse, men and women talk vehemently and superlatively, blunder and quarrel : their manners are full of desperation ; their speech is full of oaths. As soon as, with culture, things have cleared up a little, and they see them no longer in lumps and masses but accurately distributed, they desist from that weak vehemence and explain their meaning in detail. If the tongue had not been framed for articulation, man would still be a beast in the forest. The same weakness and want, on a higher plane, occurs daily in the education of ardent young men and women. ' Ah ! you don't understand me ; I have never met with any one who comprehends me : ' and they sigh and weep, write verses and walk alone, — fault of power to express their precise meaning. In a month or two, through the favor of their good genius, they meet some one so related as to assist their volcanic estate, and, good communication being once established, they are thenceforward good citizens. It is ever thus. The progress is to accuracy, to skill, to truth, from blind force.

There is a moment in the history of every nation, when, proceeding out of this brute youth, the perceptive powers reach their ripeness and have not yet become microscopic: so that man, at that instant, extends across the entire scale, and, with his feet still planted on the immense forces of night, converses by his eyes and brain with solar and stellar creation. That is the moment of adult health, the culmination of power.

Such is the history of Europe, in all points; and such in philosophy. Its early records, almost perished, are of the immigrations from Asia, bringing with them the dreams of barbarians; a confusion of crude notions of morals and of natural philosophy, gradually subsiding through the partial insight of single teachers.

Before Pericles came the Seven Wise Masters, and we have the beginnings of geometry, metaphysics and ethics : then the partialists, — deducing the origin of things from flux or water, or from air, or from fire, or from mind. All mix with these causes mythologic pictures. At last comes Plato, the distributor, who needs no barbaric paint, or tattoo, or whooping; for he can define. He leaves with Asia the vast and superlative ; he is

the arrival of accuracy and intelligence. " He
shall be as a god to me, who can rightly divide
and define."

This defining is philosophy. Philosophy is the
account which the human mind gives to itself of
the constitution of the world. Two cardinal facts
lie forever at the base ; the one, and the two. —
1. Unity, or Identity ; and, 2. Variety. We unite
all things by perceiving the law which pervades
them ; by perceiving the superficial differences and
the profound resemblances. But every mental
act, — this very perception of identity or oneness,
recognizes the difference of things. Oneness and
otherness. It is impossible to speak or to think
without embracing both.

The mind is urged to ask for one cause of many
effects ; then for the cause of that ; and again the
cause, diving still into the profound : self-assured
that it shall arrive at an absolute and sufficient
one, — a one that shall be all. " In the midst of
the sun is the light, in the midst of the light is
truth, and in the midst of truth is the imperishable
being," say the Vedas. All philosophy, of East
and West, has the same centripetence. Urged by
an opposite necessity, the mind returns from the
one to that which is not one, but other or many ;
from cause to effect ; and affirms the necessary
existence of variety, the self-existence of both, as

each is involved in the other. These strictly-blended elements it is the problem of thought to separate and to reconcile. Their existence is mutually contradictory and exclusive; and each so fast slides into the other that we can never say what is one, and what it is not. The Proteus is as nimble in the highest as in the lowest grounds; when we contemplate the one, the true, the good, — as in the surfaces and extremities of matter.

In all nations there are minds which incline to dwell in the conception of the fundamental Unity. The raptures of prayer and ecstasy of devotion lose all being in one Being. This tendency finds its highest expression in the religious writings of the East, and chiefly in the Indian Scriptures, in the Vedas, the Bhagavat Geeta, and the Vishnu Purana. Those writings contain little else than this idea, and they rise to pure and sublime strains in celebrating it.

The Same, the Same: friend and foe are of one stuff; the ploughman, the plough and the furrow are of one stuff; and the stuff is such and so much that the variations of form are unimportant. "You are fit" (says the supreme Krishna to a sage) "to apprehend that you are not distinct from me. That which I am, thou art, and that also is this world, with its gods and heroes and mankind. Men contemplate distinctions, because they are stupefied

with ignorance." "The words *I* and *mine* constitute ignorance. What is the great end of all, you
shall now learn from me. It is soul, — one in all
bodies, pervading, uniform, perfect, preeminent
over nature, exempt from birth, growth and decay,
omnipresent, made up of true knowledge, independent, unconnected with unrealities, with name,
species and the rest, in time past, present and to
come. The knowledge that this spirit, which is
essentially one, is in one's own and in all other
bodies, is the wisdom of one who knows the unity
of things. As one diffusive air, passing through
the perforations of a flute, is distinguished as the
notes of a scale, so the nature of the Great Spirit
is single, though its forms be manifold, arising
from the consequences of acts. When the difference of the investing form, as that of god or the
rest, is destroyed, there is no distinction." "The
whole world is but a manifestation of Vishnu, who
is identical with all things, and is to be regarded
by the wise as not differing from, but as the same
as themselves. I neither am going nor coming;
nor is my dwelling in any one place; nor art thou,
thou; nor are others, others; nor am I, I." As if
he had said, 'All is for the soul, and the soul is
Vishnu; and animals and stars are transient paint-
ings; and light is whitewash; and durations are
deceptive; and form is imprisonment; and heaven

itself a decoy.' That which the soul seeks is reso
lution into being above form, out of Tartarus and
out of heaven, — liberation from nature.

If speculation tends thus to a terrific unity, in
which all things are absorbed, action tends directly
backwards to diversity. The first is the course
or gravitation of mind; the second is the power
of nature. Nature is the manifold. The unity
absorbs, and melts or reduces. Nature opens and
creates. These two principles reappear and inter-
penetrate all things, all thought; the one, the
many. One is being; the other, intellect: one is
necessity; the other, freedom: one, rest; the other,
motion: one, power; the other, distribution: one,
strength; the other, pleasure: one, consciousness;
the other, definition: one, genius; the other, talent:
one, earnestness; the other, knowledge: one, possession; the other, trade: one, caste; the other,
culture: one, king; the other, democracy: and, if
we dare carry these generalizations a step higher,
and name the last tendency of both, we might
say, that the end of the one is escape from organization, — pure science; and the end of the other
is the highest instrumentality, or use of means, or
executive deity.

Each student adheres, by temperament and by
habit, to the first or to the second of these gods of
the mind. By religion, he tends to unity; by in-

tellect, or by the senses, to the many. A too
rapid unification, and an excessive appliance to
parts and particulars, are the twin dangers of speculation.

To this partiality the history of nations corre-
sponded. The country of unity, of immovable institutions, the seat of a philosophy delighting in abstractions, of men faithful in doctrine and in practice to the idea of a deaf, unimplorable, immense
fate, is Asia; and it realizes this faith in the social
institution of caste. On the other side, the genius
of Europe is active and creative : it resists caste by
culture; its philosophy was a discipline; it is a
land of arts, inventions, trade, freedom. If the
East loved infinity, the West delighted in boundaries.

European civility is the triumph of talent, the
extension of system, the sharpened understanding,
adaptive skill, delight in forms, delight in manifestation, in comprehensible results. Pericles, Athens,
Greece, had been working in this element with the
joy of genius not yet chilled by any foresight of
the detriment of an excess. They saw before them
no sinister political economy; no ominous Malthus;
no Paris or London; no pitiless subdivision of
classes, — the doom of the pin-makers, the doom of
the weavers, of dressers, of stockingers, of carders,
of spinners, of colliers; no Ireland; no Indian

caste, superinduced by the efforts of Europe to throw it off. The understanding was in its health and prime. Art was in its splendid novelty. They cut the Pentelican marble as if it were snow, and their perfect works in architecture and sculpture seemed things of course, not more difficult than the completion of a new ship at the Medford yards, or new mills at Lowell. These things are in course, and may be taken for granted. The Roman legion, Byzantine legislation, English trade, the saloons of Versailles, the cafés of Paris, the steam-mill, steamboat, steam-coach, may all be seen in perspective; the town-meeting, the ballot-box, the newspaper and cheap press.

Meantime, Plato, in Egypt and in Eastern pilgrimages, imbibed the idea of one Deity, in which all things are absorbed. The unity of Asia and the detail of Europe; the infinitude of the Asiatic soul and the defining, result-loving, machine-making, surface-seeking, opera-going Europe, — Plato came to join, and, by contact, to enhance the energy of each. The excellence of Europe and Asia are in his brain. Metaphysics and natural philosophy expressed the genius of Europe; he substructs the religion of Asia, as the base.

In short, a balanced soul was born, perceptive of the two elements. It is as easy to be great as to be small. The reason why we do not at once believe in admirable souls is because they are not in our experience. In actual life, they are so rare as to be incredible ; but primarily there is not only no presumption against them, but the strongest presumption in favor of their appearance. But whether voices were heard in the sky, or not; whether his mother or his father dreamed that the infant man-child was the son of Apollo ; whether a swarm of bees settled on his lips, or not; — a man who could see two sides of a thing was born. The wonderful synthesis so familiar in nature ; the upper and the under side of the medal of Jove. the union of impossibilities, which reappears in every object ; its real and its ideal power, — was now also transferred entire to the consciousness of a man.

The balanced soul came. If he loved abstract truth, he saved himself by propounding the most popular of all principles, the absolute good, which rules rulers, and judges the judge. If he made transcendental distinctions, he fortified himself by drawing all his illustrations from sources disdained by orators and polite conversers ; from mares and puppies ; from pitchers and soup-ladles ; from cooks and criers ; the shops of potters, horse-doctors, butchers and fishmongers. He cannot forgive in himself a partiality, but is resolved that the two poles of thought shall appear in his statement.

His argument and his sentence are self-poised and spherical. The two poles appear; yes, and become two hands, to grasp and appropriate their own.

Every great artist has been such by synthesis. Our strength is transitional, alternating; or, shall I say, a thread of two strands. The sea-shore, sea seen from shore, shore seen from sea; the taste of two metals in contact; and our enlarged powers at the approach and at the departure of a friend; the experience of poetic creativeness, which is not found in staying at home, nor yet in travelling, but in transitions from one to the other, which must therefore be adroitly managed to present as much transitional surface as possible; this command of two elements must explain the power and the charm of Plato. Art expresses the one or the same by the different. Thought seeks to know unity in unity; poetry to show it by variety; that is, always by an object or symbol. Plato keeps the two vases, one of æther and one of pigment, at his side, and invariably uses both. Things added to things, as statistics, civil history, are inventories. Things used as language are inexhaustibly attractive. Plato turns incessantly the obverse and the reverse of the medal of Jove.

To take an example: — The physical philosophers had sketched each his theory of the world;

the theory of atoms, of fire, of flux, of spirit; theories mechanical and chemical in their genius. Plato, a master of mathematics, studious of all natural laws and causes, feels these, as second causes, to be no theories of the world but bare inventories and lists. To the study of nature he therefore prefixes the dogma, — "Let us declare the cause which led the Supreme Ordainer to produce and compose the universe. He was good; and he who is good has no kind of envy. Exempt from envy, he wished that all things should be as much as possible like himself. Whosoever, taught by wise men, shall admit this as the prime cause of the origin and foundation of the world, will be in the truth." "All things are for the sake of the good, and it is the cause of every thing beautiful." This dogma animates and impersonates his philosophy.

The synthesis which makes the character of his mind appears in all his talents. Where there is great compass of wit, we usually find excellencies that combine easily in the living man, but in description appear incompatible. The mind of Plato is not to be exhibited by a Chinese catalogue, but is to be apprehended by an original mind in the exercise of its original power. In him the freest abandonment is united with the precision of a geometer. His daring imagination gives him the more solid grasp of facts; as the birds of highest flight have the strongest alar bones. His patrician polish, his intrinsic elegance, edged by an irony so subtle that it stings and paralyzes, adorn the soundest health and strength of frame. According to the old sentence, "If Jove should descend to the earth, he would speak in the style of Plato."

With this palatial air there is, for the direct aim of several of his works and running through the tenor of them all, a certain earnestness, which mounts, in the Republic and in the Phædo, to piety. He has been charged with feigning sickness at the time of the death of Socrates. But the anecdotes that have come down from the times attest his manly interference before the people in his master's behalf, since even the savage cry of the assembly to Plato is preserved; and the indignation towards popular government, in many of his pieces, expresses a personal exasperation. He has a probity, a native reverence for justice and honor, and a humanity which makes him tender for the superstitions of the people. Add to this, he believes that poetry, prophecy and the high insight are from a wisdom of which man is not master; that the gods never philosophize, but by a celestial mania these miracles are accomplished. Horsed on these winged steeds, he sweeps the dim regions, visits worlds which flesh cannot enter; he saw the souls in pain, he hears the doom of the judge, he beholds the penal metempsychosis, the Fates, with the rock and shears, and hears the intoxicating hum of their spindle.

But his circumspection never forsook him. One would say he had read the inscription on the gates of Busyrane, — "Be bold;" and on the second gate, — "Be bold, be bold, and evermore be bold;" and then again had paused well at the third gate, — "Be not too bold." His strength is like the momentum of a falling planet, and his discretion the return of its due and perfect curve, — so excellent is his Greek love of boundary and his skill in definition. In reading logarithms one is not more secure than in following Plato in his flights. Nothing can be colder than his head, when the lightnings of his imagination are playing in the sky. He has finished his thinking before he brings it to the reader, and he abounds in the surprises of a literary master. He has that opulence which furnishes, at every turn, the precise weapon he needs. As the rich man wears no more garments, drives no more horses, sits in no more chambers than the poor, — but has that one dress, or equipage, or instrument, which is fit for the hour and the need; so Plato, in his plenty, is never restricted, but has the fit word. There is indeed no weapon in all the armory of wit which he did not possess and use, — epic, analysis, mania, intuition, music, satire and irony, down to the customary and polite. His illustrations are poetry and his jests illustrations. Socrates' profession of obstetric art is good philosophy; and his finding that word "cookery," and "adulatory art," for rhetoric, in the Gorgias, does us a substantial service still. No orator can measure in effect with him who can give good nicknames.

What moderation and understatement and checking his thunder in mid volley! He has good-naturedly furnished the courtier and citizen with all that can be said against the schools. "For philosophy is an elegant thing, if any one modestly meddles with it; but if he is conversant with it more than is becoming, it corrupts the man." He could well afford to be generous, — he, who from the sunlike centrality and reach of his vision, had a faith without cloud. Such as his perception, was his speech: he plays with the doubt and makes the most of it: he paints and quibbles; and by and by comes a sentence that moves the sea and land. The admirable earnest comes not only at intervals, in the perfect yes and no of the dialogue, but in bursts of light. "I, therefore, Callicles, am persuaded by these accounts, and consider how I may exhibit my soul before the judge in a healthy condition. Wherefore, disregarding the honors that most men value, and looking to the truth, I shall endeavor in reality to live as virtuously as I can ; and when I die, to die so. And I invite all other men, to the utmost of my power ; and you too I in turn invite to this contest, which, I affirm, surpasses all contests here."

He is a great average man ; one who, to the best thinking, adds a proportion and equality in his faculties, so that men see in him their own dreams and glimpses made available and made to pass for what they are. A great common-sense is his warrant and qualification to be the world's interpreter. He has reason, as all the philosophic and poetic class have : but he has also what they have not, — this strong solving sense to reconcile his poetry with the appearances of the world, and build a bridge from the streets of cities to the Atlantis. He omits never this graduation, but slopes his thought, however picturesque the precipice on one side, to an access from the plain. He never writes in ecstacy, or catches us up into poetic raptures.

Plato apprehended the cardinal facts. He could prostrate himself on the earth and cover his eyes whilst he adored that which cannot be numbered, or gauged, or known, or named : that of which every thing can be affirmed and denied : that "which is entity and nonentity." He called it super-essential. He even stood ready, as in the

Parmenides, to demonstrate that it was so,— that this Being exceeded the limits of intellect. No man ever more fully acknowledged the Ineffable. Having paid his homage, as for the human race, to the Illimitable, he then stood erect, and for the human race affirmed, 'And yet things are knowable!'— that is, the Asia in his mind was first heartily honored, — the ocean of love and power, before form, before will, before knowledge, the Same, the Good, the One; and now, refreshed and empowered by this worship, the instinct of Europe, namely, culture, returns; and he cries, 'Yet things are knowable!' They are knowable, because being from one, things correspond. There is a scale; and the correspondence of heaven to earth, of matter to mind, of the part to the whole, is our guide. As there is a science of stars, called astronomy; a science of quantities, called mathematics; a science of qualities, called chemistry; so there is a science of sciences,— I call it Dialectic, — which is the Intellect discriminating the false and the true. It rests on the observation of identity and diversity; for to judge is to unite to an object the notion which belongs to it. The sciences, even the best,— mathematics and astronomy, — are like sportsmen, who seize whatever prey offers, even without being able to make any use of it. Dialectic must teach the use of them. "This is of that rank that no intellectual man will enter on any study for its own sake, but only with a view to advance himself in that one sole science which embraces all."

"The essence or peculiarity of man is to comprehend a whole; or that which in the diversity of sensations can be comprised under a rational unity." "The soul which has never perceived the truth, cannot pass into the human form." I announce to men the Intellect. I announce the good of being interpenetrated by the mind that made nature: this benefit, namely, that it can understand nature, which it made and maketh. Nature is good, but intellect is better: as the law-giver is before the law-receiver. I give you joy, O sons of men! that truth is altogether wholesome; that we have hope to search out what might be the very self of everything. The misery of man is to be baulked of the sight of essence and to be stuffed with conjectures; but the supreme good is reality; the supreme beauty is reality; and all virtue and all felicity depend on this science of the real: for courage is nothing else than knowledge; the fairest fortune that can befall man is to be guided by his dæmon to that which is truly his own. This also is the essence of justice, — to attend every one his own: nay, the notion of virtue is not to be arrived at except through direct contemplation of the divine essence. Courage then! for " the persuasion that we must search that which we do not know, will render us, beyond comparison, better, braver and more industrious than if we thought it impossible to discover what we do not know, and useless to search for it." He secures a position not to be commanded, by his passion for reality; valuing philosophy only as it is the pleasure of conversing with real being.

Thus, full of the genius of Europe, he said, *Culture*. He saw the institutions of Sparta and recognized, more genially one would say than any since, the hope of education. He delighted in every accomplishment, in every graceful and useful and truthful performance; above all in the splendors of genius and intellectual achievement. " The whole of life, O Socrates," said Glauco, " is, with the wise, the measure of hearing such discourses as these." What a price he sets on the feats of talent, on the powers of Pericles, of Isocrates, of Parmenides! What price above price on the talents themselves! He called the several faculties, gods, in his beautiful personation. What value he gives to the art of gymnastic in education; what to geometry; what to music; what to astronomy, whose appeasing and medicinal power he celebrates! In the Timæus he indicates the highest employment of the eyes. "By us it is asserted that God invented and bestowed sight on us for this purpose, — that on surveying the circles of intelligence in the heavens, we might properly employ those of our own minds, which, though disturbed when compared with the others that are uniform, are still allied to their circulations; and that having thus learned, and being naturally possessed of a correct reasoning faculty, we might, by imitating the uniform revolutions of divinity, set right our own wanderings and blunders." And in the Republic, — "By each of these disciplines a certain organ of the soul is both purified and reanimated which is blinded and buried by studies of another kind; an organ better worth saving than ten thousand eyes, since truth is perceived by this alone."

He said, Culture; but he first admitted its basis, and gave immeasurably the first place to advantages of nature. His patrician tastes laid stress on the distinctions of birth. In the doctrine of the organic character and disposition is the origin of caste. "Such as were fit to govern, into their composition the informing Deity mingled gold; into the military, silver; iron and brass for husbandmen and artificers." The East confirms itself, in all ages, in this faith. The Koran is explicit on this point of caste. "Men have their metal, as of gold and silver. Those of you who were the worthy

Fitz Memorial Library

Endicott Junior College

Beverly, Massachusetts 01915

ones in the state of ignorance, will be the worthy ones in the state of faith, as soon as you embrace it." Plato was not less firm. "Of the five orders of things, only four can be taught to the generality of men." In the Republic he insists on the temperaments of the youth, as first of the first.

A happier example of the stress laid on nature is in the dialogue with the young Theages, who wishes to receive lessons from Socrates. Socrates declares that if some have grown wise by associating with him, no thanks are due to him; but, simply, whilst they were with him they grew wise, not because of him; he pretends not to know the way of it. "It is adverse to many, nor can those be benefited by associating with me whom the Dæmon opposes; so that it is not possible for me to live with these. With many however he does not prevent me from conversing, who yet are not at all benefited by associating with me. Such, O Theages, is the association with me; for, if it pleases the God, you will make great and rapid proficiency: you will not, if he does not please. Judge whether it is not safer to be instructed by some one of those who have power over the benefit which they impart to men, than by me, who benefit or not, just as it may happen." As if he had said, 'I have no system. I cannot be answerable for you. You will be what you must. If there is love between

us, inconceivably delicious and profitable will our
intercourse be ; if not, your time is lost and you
will only annoy me. I shall seem to you stupid,
and the reputation I have, false. Quite above us,
beyond the will of you or me, is this secret affinity
or repulsion laid. All my good is magnetic, and
I educate, not by lessons, but by going about my
business.'

He said, Culture; he said, Nature; and he failed
not to add, ' There is also the divine.' There is
no thought in any mind but it quickly tends to
convert itself into a power and organizes a huge
instrumentality of means. Plato, lover of limits,
loved the illimitable, saw the enlargement and nobility which come from truth itself and good itself,
and attempted as if on the part of the human intellect, once for all to do it adequate homage, —
homage fit for the immense soul to receive, and yet
homage becoming the intellect to render. He said
then ' Our faculties run out into infinity, and return to us thence. We can define but a little way;
but here is a fact which will not be skipped, and
which to shut our eyes upon is suicide. All things
are in a scale; and, begin where we will, ascend
and ascend. All things are symbolical; and what
we call results are beginnings.'

A key to the method and completeness of Plato
is his twice bisected line. After he has illustrated

the relation between the absolute good and true
and the forms of the intelligible world, he says: —
" Let there be a line cut in two unequal parts.
Cut again each of these two main parts, — one
representing the visible, the other the intelligible
world, — and let these two new sections represent
the bright part and the dark part of each of these
worlds. You will have, for one of the sections of
the visible world, images, that is, both shadows and
reflections; — for the other section, the objects of
these images, that is, plants, animals, and the works
of art and nature. Then divide the intelligible
world in like manner; the one section will be of
opinions and hypotheses, and the other section of
truths." To these four sections, the four opera-
tions of the soul correspond, — conjecture, faith,
understanding, reason. As every pool reflects the
image of the sun, so every thought and thing re-
stores us an image and creature of the supreme
Good. The universe is perforated by a million
channels for his activity. All things mount and
mount.

All his thought has this ascension; in Phædrus,
teaching that beauty is the most lovely of all
things, exciting hilarity and shedding desire and
confidence through the universe wherever it enters, and it enters in some degree into all things:
— but that there is another, which is as much

more beautiful than beauty as beauty is than chaos ; namely, wisdom, which our wonderful organ of sight cannot reach unto, but which, could it be seen, would ravish us with its perfect reality. He has the same regard to it as the source of excellence in works of art. When an artificer, he says, in the fabrication of any work, looks to that which always subsists according *to the same ;* and, employing a model of this kind, expresses its idea and power in his work, — it must follow that his production should be beautiful. But when he beholds that which is born and dies, it will be far from beautiful.

Thus ever : the Banquet is a teaching in the same spirit, familiar now to all the poetry and to all the sermons of the world, that the love of the sexes is initial, and symbolizes at a distance the passion of the soul for that immense lake of beauty it exists to seek. This faith in the Divinity is never out of mind, and constitutes the ground of all his dogmas. Body cannot teach wisdom ; — God only. In the same mind he constantly affirms that virtue cannot be taught ; that it is not a science, but an inspiration ; that the greatest goods are produced to us through mania and are assigned to us by a divine gift.

This leads me to that central figure which he has established in his Academy as the organ through which every considered opinion shall be announced, and whose biography he has likewise so labored that the historic facts are lost in the light of Plato's mind. Socrates and Plato are the double star which the most powerful instruments will not entirely separate. Socrates again, in his traits and genius, is the best example of that synthesis which constitutes Plato's extraordinary power. Socrates, a man of humble stem, but honest enough; of the commonest history; of a personal homeliness so remarkable as to be a cause of wit in others: — the rather that his broad good nature and exquisite taste for a joke invited the sally, which was sure to be paid. The players personated him on the stage; the potters copied his ugly face on their stone jugs. He was a cool fellow, adding to his humor a perfect temper and a knowledge of his man, be he who he might whom he talked with, which laid the companion open to certain defeat in any debate, — and in debate he immoderately delighted. The young men are prodigiously fond of him and invite him to their feasts, whither he goes for conversation. He can drink, too; has the strongest head in Athens; and after leaving the whole party under the table, goes away as if nothing had happened, to begin new dialogues with somebody that is sober. In short, he was what our country-people call *an old one.*

He affected a good many citizen-like tastes, was
monstrously fond of Athens, hated trees, never
willingly went beyond the walls, knew the old
characters, valued the bores and philistines, thought
every thing in Athens a little better than anything
in any other place.   He was plain as a Quaker in
habit and speech, affected low phrases, and illustrations from cocks and quails, soup-pans and syca-
more-spoons, grooms and farriers, and unnameable
offices, — especially if he talked with any superfine
person.   He had a Franklin-like wisdom.   Thus
he showed one who was afraid to go on foot to
Olympia, that it was no more than his daily walk
within doors, if continuously extended, would easily
reach.

Plain old uncle as he was, with his great ears,
an immense talker, — the rumor ran that on one
or two occasions, in the war with Bœotia, he had
shown a determination which had covered the retreat of a troop ; and there was some story that
under cover of folly, he had, in the city government, when one day he chanced to hold a seat
there, evinced a courage in opposing singly the
popular voice, which had well-nigh ruined him.
He is very poor ; but then he is hardy as a soldier,
and can live on a few olives ; usually, in the strict-
est sense, on bread and water, except when entertained by his friends.   His necessary expenses

were exceedingly small, and no one could live as he did. He wore no under garment; his upper garment was the same for summer and winter, and he went barefooted; and it is said that to procure the pleasure, which he loves, of talking at his ease all day with the most elegant and cultivated young men, he will now and then return to his shop and carve statues, good or bad, for sale. However that be, it is certain that he had grown to delight in nothing else than this conversation; and that, under his hypocritical pretence of knowing nothing, he attacks and brings down all the fine speakers, all the fine philosophers of Athens, whether natives or strangers from Asia Minor and the islands. Nobody can refuse to talk with him, he is so honest and really curious to know; a man who was willingly confuted if he did not speak the truth, and who willingly confuted others asserting what was false; and not less pleased when confuted than when confuting; for he thought not any evil happened to men of such a magnitude as false opinion respecting the just and unjust. A pitiless disputant, who knows nothing, but the bounds of whose conquering intelligence no man had ever reached; whose temper was imperturbable; whose dreadful logic was always leisurely and sportive; so careless and ignorant as to disarm the wariest and draw them, in the pleasantest manner, into horrible doubts and confusion. But he always knew the way out; knew it, yet would not tell it. No escape; he drives them to terrible choices by his dilemmas, and tosses the Hippiases and Gorgiases with their grand reputations, as a boy tosses his balls. The tyrannous realist! — Meno has discoursed a thousand times, at length, on virtue, before many companies, and very well, as it appeared to him; but at this moment he cannot even tell what it is, — this cramp-fish of a Socrates has so bewitched him.

This hard-headed humorist, whose strange conceits, drollery and *bonhommie* diverted the young patricians, whilst the rumor of his sayings and quibbles gets abroad every day, — turns out, in the sequel, to have a probity as invincible as his logic, and to be either insane, or at least, under cover of this play, enthusiastic in his religion. When accused before the judges of subverting the popular creed, he affirms the immortality of the soul, the future reward and punishment; and refusing to recant, in a caprice of the popular government was condemned to die, and sent to the prison. Socrates entered the prison and took away all ignominy from the place, which could not be a prison whilst he was there. Crito bribed the jailer; but Socrates would not go out by treachery. " Whatever inconvenience ensue, nothing is to be preferred before justice. These things I hear like pipes and drums, whose sound makes me deaf to every thing you say." The fame of this prison, the fame of the discourses there and the drinking of the hemlock are one of the most precious passages in the history of the world.

The rare coincidence, in one ugly body, of the droll and the martyr, the keen street and market debater with the sweetest saint known to any history at that time, had forcibly struck the mind of Plato, so capacious of these contrasts; and the figure of Socrates by a necessity placed itself in the foreground of the scene, as the fittest dispenser of the intellectual treasures he had to communicate. It was a rare fortune that this Æsop of the mob and this robed scholar should meet, to make each other immortal in their mutual faculty. The strange synthesis in the character of Socrates capped the synthesis in the mind of Plato. Moreover by this means he was able, in the direct way and without envy to avail himself of the wit and weight of Socrates, to which unquestionably his own debt was great; and these derived again their principal advantage from the perfect art of Plato.

It remains to say that the defect of Plato in power is only that which results inevitably from his quality. He is intellectual in his aim; and therefore, in expression, literary. Mounting into heaven, diving into the pit, expounding the laws of the state, the passion of love, the remorse of crime, the hope of the parting soul, — he is literary, and never otherwise. It is almost the sole deduction from the merit of Plato that his writings have not, — what is no doubt incident to this regnancy of intellect in his work, — the vital authority which the screams of prophets and the sermons of unlettered Arabs and Jews possess. There is an interval; and to cohesion, contact is necessary.

I know not what can be said in reply to this criticism but that we have come to a fact in the nature of things: an oak is not an orange. The qualities of sugar remain with sugar, and those of salt with salt.

In the second place, he has not a system. The dearest defenders and disciples are at fault. He attempted a theory of the universe, and his theory is not complete or self-evident. One man thinks he means this, and another that; he has said one thing in one place, and the reverse of it in another place. He is charged with having failed to make the transition from ideas to matter. Here is the world, sound as a nut, perfect, not the smallest piece of chaos left, never a stitch nor an end, not a mark of haste, or botching, or second thought; but the theory of the world is a thing of shreds and patches.

The longest wave is quickly lost in the sea.

Plato would willingly have a Platonism, a known and accurate expression for the world, and it should be accurate. It shall be the world passed through the mind of Plato, — nothing less. Every atom shall have the Platonic tinge; every atom, every relation or quality you knew before, you shall know again and find here, but now ordered; not nature, but art. And you shall feel that Alexander indeed overran, with men and horses, some countries of the planet; but countries, and things of which countries are made, elements, planet itself, laws of planet and of men, have passed through this man as bread into his body, and become no longer bread, but body: so all this mammoth morsel has become Plato. He has clapped copyright on the world. This is the ambition of individualism. But the mouthful proves too large. *Boa constrictor* has good will to eat it, but he is foiled. He falls abroad in the attempt; and biting, gets strangled: the bitten world holds the biter fast by his own teeth. There he perishes: unconquered nature lives on and forgets him. So it fares with all: so must it fare with Plato. In view of eternal nature, Plato turns out to be philosophical exercitations. He argues on this side and on that. The acutest German, the lovingest disciple, could never tell what Platonism was; indeed, admirable texts can be quoted on both sides of every great question from him.

These things we are forced to say if we must consider the effort of Plato or of any philosopher to dispose of nature, — which will not be disposed of. No power of genius has ever yet had the smallest success in explaining existence. The perfect enigma remains. But there is an injustice in assuming this ambition for Plato. Let us not seem to treat with flippancy his venerable name. Men, in proportion to their intellect, have admitted his transcendent claims. The way to know him is to compare him, not with nature, but with other men. How many ages have gone by, and he remains unapproached! A chief structure of human wit, like Karnac, or the mediæval cathedrals, or the Etrurian remains, it requires all the breath of human faculty to know it. I think it is trueliest seen when seen with the most respect. His sense deepens, his merits multiply, with study. When we say, Here is a fine collection of fables; or when we praise the style, or the common sense, or arithmetic, we speak as boys, and much of our impatient criticism of the dialectic, I suspect, is no better.

The criticism is like our impatience of miles, when we are in a hurry; but it is still best that a mile should have seventeen hundred and sixty yards. The great - eyed Plato proportioned the lights and shades after the genius of our life.

PLATO: NEW READINGS.

———◆———

THE publication, in Mr. Bohn's "Serial Library," of the excellent translations of Plato, which we esteem one of the chief benefits the cheap press has yielded, gives us an occasion to take hastily a few more notes of the elevation and bearings of this fixed star; or to add a bulletin, like the journals, of *Plato at the latest dates*.

Modern science, by the extent of its generalization, has learned to indemnify the student of man for the defects of individuals by tracing growth and ascent in races; and, by the simple expedient of lighting up the vast background, generates a feeling of complacency and hope. The human being has the saurian and the plant in his rear. His arts and sciences, the easy issue of his brain, look glorious when prospectively beheld from the distant brain of ox, crocodile and fish. It seems as if nature, in regarding the geologic night behind her, when, in five or six millenniums, she had turned out five or six men, as Homer, Phidias, Menu and

Columbus, was no wise discontented with the result. These samples attested the virtue of the tree. These were a clear amelioration of trilobite and saurus, and a good basis for further proceeding. With this artist, time and space are cheap, and she is insensible to what you say of tedious preparation. She waited tranquilly the flowing periods of paleontology, for the hour to be struck when man should arrive. Then periods must pass before the motion of the earth can be suspected; then before the map of the instincts and the cultivable powers can be drawn. But as of races, so the succession of individual men is fatal and beautiful, and Plato has the fortune in the history of mankind to mark an epoch.

Plato's fame does not stand on a syllogism, or on any masterpieces of the Socratic reasoning, or on any thesis, as for example the immortality of the soul. He is more than an expert, or a schoolman, or a geometer, or the prophet of a peculiar message. He represents the privilege of the intellect, the power, namely, of carrying up every fact to successive platforms and so disclosing in every fact a germ of expansion. These expansions are in the essence of thought. The naturalist would never help us to them by any discoveries of the extent of the universe, but is as poor when cataloguing the resolved nebula of Orion, as when

measuring the angles of an acre. But the Republic of Plato, by these expansions, may be said to
require and so to anticipate the astronomy of
Laplace. The expansions are organic. The mind
does not create what it perceives, any more than
the eye creates the rose.   In ascribing to Plato the
merit of announcing them, we only say, Here was
a more complete man, who could apply to nature
the whole scale of the senses, the understanding
and the reason. These expansions or extensions
consist in continuing the spiritual sight where the
horizon falls on our natural vision, and by this
second sight discovering the long lines of law
which shoot in every direction.   Everywhere he
stands on a path which has no end, but runs continuously round the universe.   Therefore every
word becomes an exponent of nature. Whatever
he looks upon discloses a second sense, and ulterior
senses. His perception of the generation of contraries, of death out of life and life out of death,—
that law by which, in nature, decomposition is re-
composition, and putrefaction and cholera are only
signals of a new creation ; his discernment of the
little in the large and the large in the small ;
studying the state in the citizen and the citizen
in the state ; and leaving it doubtful whether he
exhibited the Republic as an allegory on the education of the private soul ; his beautiful definitions

of ideas, of time, of form, of figure, of the line, sometimes hypothetically given, as his defining of virtue, courage, justice, temperance; his love of the apologue, and his apologues themselves; the cave of Trophonius; the ring of Gyges; the char-ioteer and two horses; the golden, silver, brass and iron temperaments; Theuth and Thamus; and the visions of Hades and the Fates,—fables which have imprinted themselves in the human memory like the signs of the zodiac; his soliform eye and his boniform soul; his doctrine of assimilation; his doctrine of reminiscence; his clear vision of the laws of return, or reaction, which secure instant justice throughout the universe, instanced every-where, but specially in the doctrine, " what comes from God to us, returns from us to God," and in Socrates' belief that the laws below are sisters of the laws above.

More striking examples are his moral conclu-sions. Plato affirms the coincidence of science and virtue; for vice can never know itself and virtue, but virtue knows both itself and vice. The eye attested that justice was best, as long as it was profitable; Plato affirms that it is profitable throughout; that the profit is intrinsic, though the just conceal his justice from gods and men; that it is better to suffer injustice than to do it; that the sinner ought to covet punishment; that the

lie was more hurtful than homicide; and that
ignorance, or the involuntary lie, was more calami-
tous than involuntary homicide; that the soul is
unwillingly deprived of true opinions, and that no
man sins willingly; that the order or proceeding
of nature was from the mind to the body, and,
though a sound body cannot restore an unsound
mind, yet a good soul can, by its virtue, render the
body the best possible. The intelligent have a
right over the ignorant, namely, the right of in-
structing them. The right punishment of one out
of tune is to make him play in tune; the fine
which the good, refusing to govern, ought to pay,
is, to be governed by a worse man; that his guards
shall not handle gold and silver, but shall be instructed that there is gold and silver in their souls,
which will make men willing to give them every
thing which they need.

This second sight explains the stress laid on
geometry. He saw that the globe of earth was
not more lawful and precise than was the supersensible; that a celestial geometry was in place
there, as a logic of lines and angles here below;
that the world was throughout mathematical; the
proportions are constant of oxygen, azote and lime;
there is just so much water and slate and magnesia;
not less are the proportions constant of the moral
elements.

This eldest Goethe, hating varnish and falsehood, delighted in revealing the real at the base
of the accidental; in discovering connection, continuity and representation everywhere, hating insu-
lation; and appears like the god of wealth among
the cabins of vagabonds, opening power and capa-
bility in everything he touches. Ethical science
was new and vacant when Plato could write thus:
— "Of all whose arguments are left to the men
of the present time, no one has ever yet condemned
injustice, or praised justice, otherwise than as respects the repute, honors and emoluments arising
therefrom; while, as respects either of them in itself, and subsisting by its own power in the soul
of the possessor, and concealed both from gods
and men, no one has yet sufficiently investigated,
either in poetry or prose writings, — how, namely,
that injustice is the greatest of all the evils that
the soul has within it, and justice the greatest
good."

His definition of ideas, as what is simple,
permanent, uniform and self-existent, forever discriminating them from the notions of the understanding, marks an era in the world. He was
born to behold the self-evolving power of spirit,
endless, generator of new ends; a power which is
the key at once to the centrality and the eva-
nescence of things. Plato is so centred that he

can well spare all his dogmas. Thus the fact of
knowledge and ideas reveals to him the fact of
eternity; and the doctrine of reminiscence he
offers as the most probable particular explication.
Call that fanciful, — it matters not: the connection between our knowledge and the abyss of
being is still real, and the explication must be
not less magnificent.

He has indicated every eminent point in speculation. He wrote on the scale of the mind
itself, so that all things have symmetry in his
tablet. He put in all the past, without weariness,
and descended into detail with a courage like
that he witnessed in nature. One would say
that his forerunners had mapped out each a farm
or a district or an island, in intellectual geog-
raphy, but that Plato first drew the sphere. He
domesticates the soul in nature: man is the microcosm. All the circles of the visible heaven represent as many circles in the rational soul. There
is no lawless particle, and there is nothing casual
in the action of the human mind. The names of
things, too, are fatal, following the nature of
things. All the gods of the Pantheon are, by
their names, significant of a profound sense. The
gods are the ideas. Pan is speech, or manifestation; Saturn, the contemplative; Jove, the regal
soul; and Mars, passion. Venus is proportion;

Calliope, the soul of the world; Aglaia, intellectual illustration.

These thoughts, in sparkles of light, had appeared often to pious and to poetic souls; but this well-bred, all-knowing Greek geometer comes with command, gathers them all up into rank and gradation, the Euclid of holiness, and marries the two parts of nature. Before all men, he saw the intellectual values of the moral sentiment. He describes his own ideal, when he paints, in Timæus, a god leading things from disorder into order. He kindled a fire so truly in the centre that we see the sphere illuminated, and can distinguish poles, equator and lines of latitude, every arc and node: a theory so averaged, so modulated, that you would say the winds of ages had swept through this rhythmic structure, and not that it was the brief extempore blotting of one short-lived scribe. Hence it has happened that a very well-marked class of souls, namely those who delight in giving a spiritual, that is, an ethico-intellectual expression to every truth, by exhibiting an ulterior end which is yet legitimate to it,— are said to Platonize. Thus, Michael Angelo is a Platonist in his sonnets: Shakspeare is a Platonist when he writes,—

> "Nature is made better by no mean,
> But nature makes that mean,"

or,—

> "He, that can endure
> To follow with allegiance a fallen lord,
> Does conquer him that did his master conquer,
> And earns a place in the story."

Hamlet is a pure Platonist, and 't is the magnitude only of Shakspeare's proper genius that hinders him from being classed as the most eminent of this school. Swedenborg, throughout his prose poem of "Conjugal Love," is a Platonist.

His subtlety commended him to men of thought. The secret of his popular success is the moral aim which endeared him to mankind. "Intellect," he said, "is king of heaven and of earth;" but in Plato, intellect is always moral. His writings have also the sempiternal youth of poetry. For their arguments, most of them, might have been couched in sonnets : and poetry has never soared higher than in the Timæus and the Phædrus. As the poet, too, he is only contemplative. He did not, like Pythagoras, break himself with an institution. All his painting in the Republic must be esteemed mythical, with intent to bring out, sometimes in violent colors, his thought. You cannot institute, without peril of charlatanism.

It was a high scheme, his absolute privilege for the best (which, to make emphatic, he expressed by community of women), as the premium which he would set on grandeur. There shall be exempts of two kinds: first, those who by demerit have put themselves below protection,—outlaws; and secondly, those who by eminence of nature and desert are out of the reach of your rewards. Let such be free of the city and above the law. We confide them to themselves; let them do with us as they will. Let none presume to measure the irregularities of Michael Angelo and Socrates by village scales.

In his eighth book of the Republic, he throws a little mathematical dust in our eyes. I am sorry to see him, after such noble superiorities, permitting the lie to governors. Plato plays Providence a little with the baser sort, as people allow themselves with their dogs and cats.

SWEDENBORG; OR, THE MYSTIC.

III.

SWEDENBORG ; OR, THE MYSTIC.

---·---

AMONG eminent persons, those who are most dear to men are not of the class which the economist calls producers : they have nothing in their hands; they have not cultivated corn, nor made bread ; they have not led out a colony, nor invented a loom. A higher class, in the estimation and love of this city-building market-going race of mankind, are the poets, who, from the intellectual kingdom, feed the thought and imagination with ideas and pictures which raise men out of the world of corn and money, and console them for the short-comings of the day and the meanness of labor and traffic. Then, also, the philosopher has his value, who flatters the intellect of this laborer by engaging him with subtleties which instruct him in new faculties. Others may build cities ; he is to understand them and keep them in awe. But there is a class who lead us into another region, — the world of morals or of will. What is singular about this region of thought is its claim. Wherever the sentiment of right comes in, it takes precedence of every thing else. For other things, I make poetry of them ; but the moral sentiment makes poetry of me.

I have sometimes thought that he would render the greatest service to modern criticism, who should draw the line of relation that subsists between Shakspeare and Swedenborg. The human mind stands ever in perplexity, demanding intellect, demanding sanctity, impatient equally of each without the other. The reconciler has not yet appeared. If we tire of the saints, Shakspeare is our city of refuge. Yet the instincts presently teach that the problem of essence must take precedence of all others ; — the questions of Whence ? What ? and Whither ? and the solution of these must be in a life, and not in a book. A drama or poem is a proximate or oblique reply ; but Moses, Menu, Jesus, work directly on this problem. The atmosphere of moral sentiment is a region of grandeur which reduces all material magnificence to toys, yet opens to every wretch that has reason the doors of the universe. Almost with a fierce haste it lays its empire on the man. In the language of the Koran, " God said, the heaven and the earth and all that is between them, think ye that we created them in jest, and that ye shall not return to us ? " It is the kingdom of the will, and by inspiring the will, which is the seat of personality, seems to convert the universe into a person ; —

> " The realms of being to no other bow,
> Not only all are thine, but all are Thou."

All men are commanded by the saint. The Koran makes a distinct class of those who are by nature good, and whose goodness has an influence on others, and pronounces this class to be the aim of creation : the other classes are admitted to the feast of being, only as following in the train of this. And the Persian poet exclaims to a soul of this kind, —

> " Go boldly forth, and feast on being's banquet;
> Thou art the called, — the rest admitted with thee."

The privilege of this caste is an access to the secrets and structure of nature by some higher method than by experience. In common parlance, what one man is said to learn by experience, a man of extraordinary sagacity is said, without experience, to divine. The Arabians say, that Abul Khain, the mystic, and Abu Ali Seena, the philosopher, conferred together ; and, on parting, the philosopher said, " All that he sees, I know ; " and the mystic said, " All that he knows, I see." If one should ask the reason of this intuition, the solution would lead us into that property which

Plato denoted as Reminiscence, and which is implied by the Bramins in the tenet of Transmigration. The soul having been often born, or, as the
Hindoos say, "travelling the path of existence
through thousands of births," having beheld the
things which are here, those which are in heaven
and those which are beneath, there is nothing of
which she has not gained the knowledge: no wonder that she is able to recollect, in regard to any
one thing, what formerly she knew. "For, all
things in nature being linked and related, and the
soul having heretofore known all, nothing hinders
but that any man who has recalled to mind, or according to the common phrase has learned, one
thing only, should of himself recover all his ancient
knowledge, and find out again all the rest, if he
have but courage and faint not in the midst of his
researches. For inquiry and learning is reminiscence all." How much more, if he that inquires
be a holy and godlike soul! For by being as-
similated to the original soul, by whom and after
whom all things subsist, the soul of man does then
easily flow into all things, and all things flow into
it: they mix; and he is present and sympathetic
with their structure and law.

This path is difficult, secret and beset with terror. The ancients called it *ecstacy* or absence, —
a getting out of their bodies to think. All relig-

ious history contains traces of the trance of saints,
— a beatitude, but without any sign of joy; earnest, solitary, even sad; "the flight," Plotinus
called it, "of the alone to the alone;" Μύησις, the
closing of the eyes, — whence our word, *Mystic.*
The trances of Socrates, Plotinus, Porphyry, Behmen, Bunyan, Fox, Pascal, Guyon, Swedenborg,
will readily come to mind. But what as readily
comes to mind is the accompaniment of disease.
This beatitude comes in terror, and with shocks to
the mind of the receiver.

> "It o'erinforms the tenement of clay,"

and drives the man mad; or gives a certain violent bias which taints his judgment. In the chief
examples of religious illumination somewhat mor-
bid has mingled, in spite of the unquestionable increase of mental power. Must the highest good
drag after it a quality which neutralizes and dis-
credits it? —

> "Indeed, it takes
> From our achievements, when performed at height,
> The pith and marrow of our attribute."

Shall we say, that the economical mother disburses
so much earth and so much fire, by weight and
meter, to make a man, and will not add a penny-
weight though a nation is perishing for a leader?
Therefore the men of God purchased their science

by folly or pain. If you will have pure carbon, carbuncle, or diamond, to make the brain transparent, the trunk and organs shall be so much the grosser: instead of porcelain they are potter's earth, clay, or mud.

In modern times no such remarkable example of this introverted mind has occurred as in Emanuel Swedenborg, born in Stockholm, in 1688. This man, who appeared to his contemporaries a visionary and elixir of moonbeams, no doubt led the most real life of any man then in the world: and now, when the royal and ducal Frederics, Christians and Brunswicks of that day have slid into oblivion, he begins to spread himself into the minds of thousands. As happens in great men, he seemed, by the variety and amount of his powers, to be a composition of several persons, — like the giant fruits which are matured in gardens by the union of four or five single blossoms. His frame is on a larger scale and possesses the advantages of size. As it is easier to see the reflection of the great sphere in large globes, though defaced by some crack or blemish, than in drops of water, so men of large calibre, though with some eccentricity or madness, like Pascal or Newton, help us more than balanced mediocre minds.

His youth and training could not fail to be extraordinary. Such a boy could not whistle or

dance, but goes grubbing into mines and mountains, prying into chemistry and optics, physiology,
mathematics and astronomy, to find images fit for
the measure of his versatile and capacious brain.
He was a scholar from a child, and was educated
at Upsala. At the age of twenty-eight he was
made Assessor of the Board of Mines by Charles
XII. In 1716, he left home for four years and
visited the universities of England, Holland,
France and Germany. He performed a notable
feat of engineering in 1718, at the siege of Fred-
erikshald, by hauling two galleys, five boats and a
sloop, some fourteen English miles overland, for
the royal service. In 1721 he journeyed over Europe to examine mines and smelting works. He
published in 1716 his Dædalus Hyperboreus, and
from this time for the next thirty years was employed in the composition and publication of his
scientific works. With the like force he threw
himself into theology. In 1743, when he was fifty-
four years old, what is called his illumination began. All his metallurgy and transportation of
ships overland was absorbed into this ecstasy. He
ceased to publish any more scientific books, with-
drew from his practical labors and devoted himself
to the writing and publication of his voluminous
theological works, which were printed at his own
expense, or at that of the Duke of Brunswick or

other prince, at Dresden, Leipsic, London, or Am-
sterdam. Later, he resigned his office of Assessor:
the salary attached to this office continued to be
paid to him during his life. His duties had
brought him into intimate acquaintance with King
Charles XII., by whom he was much consulted and
honored. The like favor was continued to him by
his successor. At the Diet of 1751, Count Hop-
ken says, the most solid memorials on finance were
from his pen. In Sweden he appears to have at-
tracted a marked regard. His rare science and
practical skill, and the added fame of second sight
and extraordinary religious knowledge and gifts,
drew to him queens, nobles, clergy, shipmasters
and people about the ports through which he was
wont to pass in his many voyages. The clergy interfered a little with the importation and publication of his religious works, but he seems to have
kept the friendship of men in power. He was
never married. He had great modesty and gentle-
ness of bearing. His habits were simple; he lived
on bread, milk and vegetables; he lived in a house
situated in a large garden; he went several times
to England, where he does not seem to have at-
tracted any attention whatever from the learned
or the eminent; and died at London, March 29,
1772, of apoplexy, in his eighty-fifth year. He is
described, when in London, as a man of a quiet,

clerical habit, not averse to tea and coffee, and kind to children. He wore a sword when in full velvet dress, and, whenever he walked out, carried a gold-headed cane. There is a common portrait of him in antique coat and wig, but the face has a wandering or vacant air.

The genius which was to penetrate the science of the age with a far more subtle science; to pass the bounds of space and time, venture into the dim spirit-realm, and attempt to establish a new relig- ion in the world, — began its lessons in quarries and forges, in the smelting-pot and crucible, in ship-yards and dissecting-rooms. No one man is perhaps able to judge of the merits of his works on so many subjects. One is glad to learn that his books on mines and metals are held in the highest esteem by those who understand these matters. It seems that he anticipated much science of the nine- teenth century; anticipated, in astronomy, the dis- covery of the seventh planet, — but, unhappily, not also of the eighth; anticipated the views of mod- ern astronomy in regard to the generation of earths by the sun; in magnetism, some important experi- ments and conclusions of later students; in chemis- try, the atomic theory; in anatomy, the discoveries of Schlichting, Monro and Wilson; and first de- monstrated the office of the lungs. His excellent English editor magnanimously lays no stress on his discoveries, since he was too great to care to be original; and we are to judge, by what he can spare, of what remains.

A colossal soul, he lies vast abroad on his times, uncomprehended by them, and requires a long focal distance to be seen; suggests, as Aristotle, Bacon, Selden, Humboldt, that a certain vastness of learning, or *quasi* omnipresence of the human soul in nature, is possible. His superb speculation, as from a tower, over nature and arts, without ever losing sight of the texture and sequence of things, almost realizes his own picture, in the " Principia," of the original integrity of man. Over and above the merit of his particular discoveries, is the capital merit of his self-equality. A drop of water has the properties of the sea, but cannot exhibit a storm. There is beauty of a concert, as well as of a flute; strength of a host, as well as of a hero; and, in Swedenborg, those who are best acquainted with modern books will most admire the merit of mass. One of the missouriums and mastodons of literature, he is not to be measured by whole colleges of ordinary scholars. His stalwart presence would flutter the gowns of an university. Our books are false by being fragmentary; their sentences are *bonmots*, and not parts of natural discourse; childish expressions of surprise or pleasure in nature; or, worse, owing a brief notoriety to

their petulance, or aversion from the order of nature ; — being some curiosity or oddity, designedly
not in harmony with nature and purposely framed
to excite surprise, as jugglers do by concealing
their means. But Swedenborg is systematic and
respective of the world in every sentence ; all the
means are orderly given ; his faculties work with
astronomic punctuality, and this admirable writing
is pure from all pertness or egotism.

Swedenborg was born into an atmosphere of
great ideas. It is hard to say what was his own :
yet his life was dignified by noblest pictures of the
universe. The robust Aristotelian method, with
its breadth and adequateness, shaming our sterile
and linear logic by its genial radiation, conversant
with series and degree, with effects and ends, skilful to discriminate power from form, essence from
accident, and opening, by its terminology and definition, high roads into nature, had trained a race of
athletic philosophers. Harvey had shown the circulation of the blood ; Gilbert had shown that the
earth was a magnet ; Descartes, taught by Gilbert's
magnet, with its vortex, spiral and polarity, had
filled Europe with the leading thought of vortical
motion, as the secret of nature. Newton, in the
year in which Swedenborg was born, published the
" Principia," and established the universal gravity.
Malpighi, following the high doctrines of Hippo-

crates, Leucippus and Lucretius, had given emphasis to the dogma that nature works in leasts,
— " tota in minimis existit natura." Unrivalled
dissectors, Swammerdam, Leuwenhoek, Winslow,
Eustachius, Heister, Vesalius, Boerhaave, had left
nothing for scalpel or microscope to reveal in human
or comparative anatomy : Linnæus, his contemporary, was affirming, in his beautiful science, that
" Nature is always like herself : " and, lastly, the
nobility of method, the largest application of principles, had been exhibited by Leibnitz and Christian Wolff, in cosmology ; whilst Locke and Grotius had drawn the moral argument. What was
left for a genius of the largest calibre but to go
over their ground and verify and unite? It is easy
to see, in these minds, the origin of Swedenborg's
studies, and the suggestion of his problems. He
had a capacity to entertain and vivify these volumes
of thought. Yet the proximity of these geniuses,
one or other of whom had introduced all his leading ideas, makes Swedenborg another example of
the difficulty, even in a highly fertile genius, of
proving originality, the first birth and annunciation
of one of the laws of nature.

He named his favorite views the doctrine of
Forms, the doctrine of Series and Degrees, the
doctrine of Influx, the doctrine of Correspondence.
His statement of these doctrines deserves to be

studied in his books. Not every man can read them, but they will reward him who can. His theologic works are valuable to illustrate these. His writings would be a sufficient library to a lonely and athletic student; and the "Economy of the Animal Kingdom" is one of those books which, by the sustained dignity of thinking, is an honor to the human race. He had studied spars and metals to some purpose. His varied and solid knowledge makes his style lustrous with points and shooting spiculæ of thought, and resembling one of those winter mornings when the air sparkles with crystals. The grandeur of the topics makes the grandeur of the style. He was apt for cosmology, because of that native perception of identity which made mere size of no account to him. In the atom of magnetic iron he saw the quality which would generate the spiral motion of sun and planet.

The thoughts in which he lived were, the universality of each law in nature; the Platonic doctrine of the scale or degrees; the version or conversion of each into other, and so the correspondence of all the parts; the fine secret that little explains large, and large, little; the centrality of man in nature, and the connection that subsists throughout all things : he saw that the human body was strictly universal, or an instrument through which the soul feeds and is fed by the whole of matter ;

so that he held, in exact antagonism to the skeptics, that "the wiser a man is, the more will he be a worshipper of the Deity." In short, he was a believer in the Identity-philosophy, which he held not idly, as the dreamers of Berlin or Boston, but which he experimented with and established through years of labor, with the heart and strength of the rudest Viking that his rough Sweden ever sent to battle.

This theory dates from the oldest philosophers, and derives perhaps its best illustration from the newest. It is this, that Nature iterates her means perpetually on successive planes. In the old aphorism, *nature is always self-similar*. In the plant, the eye or germinative point opens to a leaf, then to another leaf, with a power of transforming the leaf into radicle, stamen, pistil, petal, bract, sepal, or seed. The whole art of the plant is still to repeat leaf on leaf without end, the more or less of heat, light, moisture and food determining the form it shall assume. In the animal, nature makes a vertebra, or a spine of vertebræ, and helps herself still by a new spine, with a limited power of modifying its form,—spine on spine, to the end of the world. A poetic anatomist, in our own day, teaches that a snake, being a horizontal line, and man, being an erect line, constitute a right angle ; and between the lines of this mystical quadrant all animated beings find their place : and he assumes the hair-worm,

the span-worm, or the snake, as the type or predic-
tion of the spine. Manifestly, at the end of the
spine, Nature puts out smaller spines, as arms ; at
the end of the arms, new spines, as hands ; at the
other end, she repeats the process, as legs and feet.
At the top of the column she puts out another
spine, which doubles or loops itself over, as a span-
worm, into a ball, and forms the skull, with extremities again : the hands being now the upper jaw,
the feet the lower jaw, the fingers and toes being
represented this time by upper and lower teeth.
This new spine is destined to high uses. It is a
new man on the shoulders of the last. It can almost shed its trunk and manage to live alone, according to the Platonic idea in the Timæus.
Within it, on a higher plane, all that was done in
the trunk repeats itself. Nature recites her lesson
once more in a higher mood. The mind is a finer
body, and resumes its functions of feeding, digesting, absorbing, excluding and generating, in a new
and ethereal element. Here in the brain is all the
process of alimentation repeated, in the acquiring,
comparing, digesting and assimilating of experience. Here again is the mystery of generation repeated. In the brain are male and female faculties ; here is marriage, here is fruit. And there is
no limit to this ascending scale, but series on series. Every thing, at the end of one use, is taken

up into the next, each series punctually repeating
every organ and process of the last. We are
adapted to infinity. We are hard to please, and
love nothing which ends; and in nature is no end,
but every thing at the end of one use is lifted into
a superior, and the ascent of these things climbs
into dæmonic and celestial natures. Creative force,
like a musical composer, goes on unweariedly repeating a simple air or theme, now high, now low,
in solo, in chorus, ten thousand times reverberated,
till it fills earth and heaven with the chant.

Gravitation, as explained by Newton, is good,
but grander when we find chemistry only an extension of the law of masses into particles, and that
the atomic theory shows the action of chemistry to
be mechanical also. Metaphysics shows us a sort
of gravitation operative also in the mental phenomena; and the terrible tabulation of the French statists brings every piece of whim and humor to be
reducible also to exact numerical ratios. If one
man in twenty thousand, or in thirty thousand, eats
shoes or marries his grandmother, then in every
twenty thousand or thirty thousand is found one
man who eats shoes or marries his grandmother.
What we call gravitation, and fancy ultimate, is
one fork of a mightier stream for which we have
yet no name. Astronomy is excellent; but it must
come up into life to have its full value, and not re-

main there in globes and spaces. The globule of blood gyrates around its own axis in the human veins, as the planet in the sky; and the circles of intellect relate to those of the heavens. Each law of nature has the like universality; eating, sleep or hybernation, rotation, generation, metamorphosis, vortical motion, which is seen in eggs as in planets. These grand rhymes or returns in nature, — the dear, best-known face startling us at every turn, under a mask so unexpected that we think it the face of a stranger, and carrying up the semblance into divine forms, — delighted the prophetic eye of Swedenborg; and he must be reckoned a leader in that revolution, which, by giving to science an idea, has given to an aimless accumulation of experiments, guidance and form and a beating heart.

I own with some regret that his printed works amount to about fifty stout octavos, his scientific works being about half of the whole number; and it appears that a mass of manuscript still unedited remains in the royal library at Stockholm. The scientific works have just now been translated into English, in an excellent edition.

Swedenborg printed these scientific books in the ten years from 1734 to 1744, and they remained from that time neglected; and now, after their century is complete, he has at last found a pupil in Mr. Wilkinson, in London, a philosophic critic,

with a coequal vigor of understanding and imagination comparable only to Lord Bacon's, who has
restored his master's buried books to the day, and
transferred them, with every advantage, from their
forgotten Latin into English, to go round the world
in our commercial and conquering tongue. This
startling reappearance of Swedenborg, after a hundred years, in his pupil, is not the least remarkable
fact in his history. Aided it is said by the munifi-
cence of Mr. Clissold, and also by his literary skill,
this piece of poetic justice is done. The admirable
preliminary discourses with which Mr. Wilkinson
has enriched these volumes, throw all the contemporary philosophy of England into shade, and leave
me nothing to say on their proper grounds.

The "Animal Kingdom" is a book of wonderful merits. It was written with the highest end, —
to put science and the soul, long estranged from
each other, at one again. It was an anatomist's
account of the human body, in the highest style
of poetry. Nothing can exceed the bold and brilliant treatment of a subject usually so dry and
repulsive. He saw nature "wreathing through
an everlasting spiral, with wheels that never dry,
on axles that never creak, " and sometimes sought
" to uncover those secret recesses where Nature is
sitting at the fires in the depths of her laboratory;" whilst the picture comes recommended by

the hard fidelity with which it is based on practical anatomy. It is remarkable that this sublime genius decides peremptorily for the analytic, against the synthetic method ; and, in a book whose genius is a daring poetic synthesis, claims to confine himself to a rigid experience.

He knows, if he only, the flowing of nature, and how wise was that old answer of Amasis to him who bade him drink up the sea, — "Yes, willingly, if you will stop the rivers that flow in." Few knew as much about nature and her subtle manners, or expressed more subtly her goings. He thought as large a demand is made on our faith by nature, as by miracles. "He noted that in her proceeding from first principles through her several subordinations, there was no state through which she did not pass, as if her path lay through all things." "For as often as she betakes herself upward from visible phenomena, or, in other words, withdraws herself inward, she instantly as it were disappears, while no one knows what has become of her, or whither she is gone: so that it is necessary to take science as a guide in pursuing her steps."

The pursuing the inquiry under the light of an end or final cause gives wonderful animation, a sort of personality to the whole writing. This book announces his favorite dogmas. The ancient doctrine of Hippocrates, that the brain is a gland ;

and of Leucippus, that the atom may be known by
the mass; or, in Plato, the macrocosm by the
microcosm; and, in the verses of Lucretius, —

> Ossa videlicet e pauxillis atque minutis
> Ossibus sic et de pauxillis atque minutis
> Visceribus viscus gigni, sanguenque creari
> Sanguinis inter se multis coeuntibus guttis ;
> Ex aurique putat micis consistere posse
> Aurum, et de terris terram concrescere parvis ;
> Ignibus ex igneis, humorem humoribus esse.
>
> Lib. I. 835.

" The principle of all things, entrails made
Of smallest entrails ; bone, of smallest bone ;
Blood, of small sanguine drops reduced to one ;
Gold, of small grains ; earth, of small sands compacted ;
Small drops to water, sparks to fire contracted : "

and which Malpighi had summed in his maxim
that "nature exists entire in leasts," — is a favorite
thought of Swedenborg. " It is a constant law of
the organic body that large, compound, or visible
forms exist and subsist from smaller, simpler and
ultimately from invisible forms, which act similarly
to the larger ones, but more perfectly and more
universally; and the least forms so perfectly and
universally as to involve an idea representative of
their entire universe." The unities of each organ
are so many little organs, homogeneous with their
compound : the unities of the tongue are little
tongues; those of the stomach, little stomachs;

those of the heart are little hearts. This fruitful idea furnishes a key to every secret. What was too small for the eye to detect was read by the aggregates; what was too large, by the units. There is no end to his application of the thought. "Hunger is an aggregate of very many little hungers, or losses of blood by the little veins all over the body." It is a key to his theology also. "Man is a kind of very minute heaven, corresponding to the world of spirits and to heaven. Every particular idea of man, and every affection, yea, every smallest part of his affection, is an image and effigy of him. A spirit may be known from only a single thought. God is the grand man."

The hardihood and thoroughness of his study of nature required a theory of forms also. "Forms ascend in order from the lowest to the highest. The lowest form is angular, or the terrestrial and corporeal. The second and next higher form is the circular, which is also called the perpetual-angular, because the circumference of a circle is a perpetual angle. The form above this is the spiral, parent and measure of circular forms: its diameters are not rectilinear, but variously circular, and have a spherical surface for centre; therefore it is called the perpetual-circular. The form above this is the vortical, or perpetual-spiral: next, the perpetual-vortical, or celestial: last, the perpetual-celestial, or spiritual."

Was it strange that a genius so bold should take the last step also, should conceive that he might attain the science of all sciences, to unlock the meaning of the world? In the first volume of the "Animal Kingdom," he broaches the subject in a remarkable note:—" In our doctrine of Representations and Correspondences we shall treat of both these symbolical and typical resemblances, and of the astonishing things which occur, I will not say in the living body only, but throughout nature, and which correspond so entirely to supreme and spiritual things that one would swear that the physical world was purely symbolical of the spiritual world; insomuch that if we choose to express any natural truth in physical and definite vocal terms, and to convert these terms only into the corresponding and spiritual terms, we shall by this means elicit a spiritual truth or theological dogma, in place of the physical truth or precept: although no mortal would have predicted that any thing of the kind could possibly arise by bare literal transposition; inasmuch as the one precept, considered separately from the other, appears to have absolutely no relation to it. I intend hereafter to communicate a number of examples of such correspondences, together with a vocabulary containing the terms of spiritual things, as well as of the physical things for which they are to be substituted. This symbolism pervades the living body."

The fact thus explicitly stated is implied in all poetry, in allegory, in fable, in the use of emblems and in the structure of language. Plato knew it, as is evident from his twice bisected line in the sixth book of the Republic. Lord Bacon had found that truth and nature differed only as seal and print; and he instanced some physical propositions, with their translation into a moral or political sense. Behmen, and all mystics, imply this law in their dark riddle-writing. The poets, in as far as they are poets, use it; but it is known to them only as the magnet was known for ages, as a toy. Swedenborg first put the fact into a detached and scientific statement, because it was habitually present to him, and never not seen. It was involved, as we explained already, in the doctrine of identity and iteration, because the mental series exactly tallies with the material series. It required an insight that could rank things in order and series; or rather it required such rightness of position that the poles of the eye should coincide with the axis of the world. The earth had fed its mankind through five or six millenniums, and they had sciences, religions, philosophies, and yet had failed to see the correspondence of meaning between every part and every other part. And, down to this hour, literature has no book in which the symbolism of things is scientifically opened. One

would say that as soon as men had the first hint
that every sensible object, — animal, rock, river, air,
— nay, space and time, subsists not for itself, nor
finally to a material end, but as a picture-language
to tell another story of beings and duties, other
science would be put by, and a science of such
grand presage would absorb all faculties: that each
man would ask of all objects what they mean:
Why does the horizon hold me fast, with my joy
and grief, in this centre? Why hear I the same
sense from countless differing voices, and read one
never quite expressed fact in endless picture-language? Yet whether it be that these things will
not be intellectually learned, or that many centuries must elaborate and compose so rare and opu-
lent a soul, — there is no comet, rock-stratum, fos-
sil, fish, quadruped, spider, or fungus, that, for
itself, does not interest more scholars and classi-
fiers than the meaning and upshot of the frame of
things.

But Swedenborg was not content with the culi-
nary use of the world. In his fifty-fourth year
these thoughts held him fast, and his profound
mind admitted the perilous opinion, too frequent
in religious history, that he was an abnormal person, to whom was granted the privilege of conversing with angels and spirits ; and this ecstasy connected itself with just this office of explaining the

moral import of the sensible world. To a right
perception, at once broad and minute, of the order
of nature, he added the comprehension of the
moral laws in their widest social aspects; but whatever he saw, through some excessive determination
to form in his constitution, he saw not abstractly,
but in pictures, heard it in dialogues, constructed
it in events. When he attempted to announce the
law most sanely, he was forced to couch it in para-
ble.

Modern psychology offers no similar example of
a deranged balance. The principal powers continued to maintain a healthy action, and to a reader
who can make due allowance in the report for the
reporter's peculiarities, the results are still instructive, and a more striking testimony to the sublime
laws he announced than any that balanced dulness
could afford. He attempts to give some account
of the *modus* of the new state, affirming that "his
presence in the spiritual world is attended with a
certain separation, but only as to the intellectual
part of his mind, not as to the will part;" and he
affirms that "he sees, with the internal sight, the
things that are in another life, more clearly than
he sees the things which are here in the world."

Having adopted the belief that certain books of
the Old and New Testaments were exact allegories,
or written in the angelic and ecstatic mode, he em-

ployed his remaining years in extricating from the
literal, the universal sense. He had borrowed from
Plato the fine fable of "a most ancient people, men
better than we and dwelling nigher to the gods;"
and Swedenborg added that they used the earth
symbolically; that these, when they saw terrestrial
objects, did not think at all about them, but only
about those which they signified. The correspondence between thoughts and things henceforward occupied him. "The very organic form resembles
the end inscribed on it." A man is in general and
in particular an organized justice or injustice, selfishness or gratitude. And the cause of this harmony he assigned in the Arcana: "The reason
why all and single things, in the heavens and on
earth, are representative, is because they exist from
an influx of the Lord, through heaven." This design of exhibiting such correspondences, which, if
adequately executed, would be the poem of the
world, in which all history and science would play
an essential part, was narrowed and defeated by
the exclusively theologic direction which his in-
quiries took. His perception of nature is not human and universal, but is mystical and Hebraic.
He fastens each natural object to a theologic notion; — a horse signifies carnal understanding; a
tree, perception; the moon, faith; a cat means
this; an ostrich that; an artichoke this other; —

and poorly tethers every symbol to a several ec-
clesiastic sense. The slippery Proteus is not so
easily caught. In nature, each individual symbol
plays innumerable parts, as each particle of matter
circulates in turn through every system. The central identity enables any one symbol to express successively all the qualities and shades of real being.
In the transmission of the heavenly waters, every
hose fits every hydrant. Nature avenges herself
speedily on the hard pedantry that would chain her
waves. She is no literalist. Every thing must be
taken genially, and we must be at the top of our
condition to understand any thing rightly.

His theological bias thus fatally narrowed his
interpretation of nature, and the dictionary of symbols is yet to be written. But the interpreter
whom mankind must still expect, will find no pre-
decessor who has approached so near to the true
problem.

Swedenborg styles himself in the title-page of
his books, " Servant of the Lord Jesus Christ ; "
and by force of intellect, and in effect, he is the
last Father in the Church, and is not likely to have
a successor. No wonder that his depth of ethical
wisdom should give him influence as a teacher.
To the withered traditional church, yielding dry
catechisms, he let in nature again, and the worshipper, escaping from the vestry of verbs and texts, is

surprised to find himself a party to the whole of
his religion. His religion thinks for him and is of
universal application. He turns it on every side ;
it fits every part of life, interprets and dignifies
every circumstance. Instead of a religion which
visited him diplomatically three or four times, —
when he was born, when he married, when he fell
sick and when he died, and, for the rest, never interfered with him, — here was a teaching which
accompanied him all day, accompanied him even
into sleep and dreams ; into his thinking, and
showed him through what a long ancestry his
thoughts descend ; into society, and showed by
what affinities he was girt to his equals and his
counterparts ; into natural objects, and showed
their origin and meaning, what are friendly, and
what are hurtful ; and opened the future world
by indicating the continuity of the same laws.
His disciples allege that their intellect is invigor-
ated by the study of his books.

There is no such problem for criticism as his
theological writings, their merits are so commanding, yet such grave deductions must be made.
Their immense and sandy diffuseness is like the
prairie or the desert, and their incongruities are
like the last deliration. He is superfluously explan-
atory, and his feeling of the ignorance of men,
strangely exaggerated. Men take truths of this

nature very fast. Yet he abounds in assertions, he is a rich discoverer, and of things which most import us to know. His thought dwells in essential resemblances, like the resemblance of a house to the man who built it. He saw things in their law, in likeness of function, not of structure. There is an invariable method and order in his delivery of his truth, the habitual proceeding of the mind from inmost to outmost. What earnestness and weightiness, — his eye never roving, without one swell of vanity, or one look to self in any common form of literary pride! a theoretic or speculative man, but whom no practical man in the universe could affect to scorn. Plato is a gownsman; his garment, though of purple, and almost sky-woven, is an academic robe and hinders action with its voluminous folds. But this mystic is awful to Cæsar. Lycurgus himself would bow.

The moral insight of Swedenborg, the correction of popular errors, the announcement of ethical laws, take him out of comparison with any other modern writer and entitle him to a place, vacant for some ages, among the lawgivers of mankind. That slow but commanding influence which he has acquired, like that of other religious geniuses, must be excessive also, and have its tides, before it subsides into a permanent amount. Of course what is real and universal cannot be confined to the circle of those who sympathize strictly with his genius, but will pass forth into the common stock of wise and just thinking. The world has a sure chemistry, by which it extracts what is excellent in its children and lets fall the infirmities and limitations of the grandest mind.

That metempsychosis which is familiar in the old mythology of the Greeks, collected in Ovid and in the Indian Transmigration, and is there *objective*, or really takes place in bodies by alien will,— in Swedenborg's mind has a more philosophic character. It is subjective, or depends entirely upon the thought of the person. All things in the universe arrange themselves to each person anew, according to his ruling love. Man is such as his affection and thought are. Man is man by virtue of willing, not by virtue of knowing and understanding. As he is, so he sees. The marriages of the world are broken up. Interiors associate all in the spiritual world. Whatever the angels looked upon was to them celestial. Each Satan appears to himself a man; to those as bad as he, a comely man; to the purified, a heap of carrion. Nothing can resist states: every thing gravitates: like will to like: what we call poetic justice takes effect on the spot. We have come into a world which is a living poem. Every thing is as I am. Bird and beast is not bird and

beast, but emanation and effluvia of the minds
and wills of men there present. Every one makes
his own house and state. The ghosts are tor-
mented with the fear of death and cannot remember that they have died. They who are in evil
and falsehood are afraid of all others. Such as
have deprived themselves of charity, wander and
flee : the societies which they approach discover
their quality and drive them away. The covet-
ous seem to themselves to be abiding in cells
where their money is deposited, and these to be
infested with mice. They who place merit in
good works seem to themselves to cut wood. " I
asked such, if they were not wearied ? They re-
plied, that they have not yet done work enough
to merit heaven."

He delivers golden sayings which express with
singular beauty the ethical laws ; as when he
uttered that famed sentence, that " In heaven the
angels are advancing continually to the spring-
time of their youth, so that the oldest angel appears the youngest : " " The more angels, the
more room : " " The perfection of man is the love
of use : " " Man, in his perfect form, is heaven : "
" What is from Him, is Him : " " Ends always
ascend as nature descends." And the truly poetic
account of the writing in the inmost heaven, which,
as it consists of inflexions according to the form

of heaven, can be read without instruction. He
almost justifies his claim to preternatural vision,
by strange insights of the structure of the human
body and mind. "It is never permitted to any
one, in heaven, to stand behind another and look
at the back of his head; for then the influx which
is from the Lord is disturbed." The angels, from
the sound of the voice, know a man's love; from
the articulation of the sound, his wisdom; and
from the sense of the words, his science.

In the "Conjugal Love," he has unfolded the
science of marriage. Of this book one would say
that with the highest elements it has failed of
success. It came near to be the Hymn of Love,
which Plato attempted in the "Banquet;" the
love, which, Dante says, Casella sang among the
angels in Paradise; and which, as rightly celebrated, in its genesis, fruition and effect, might
well entrance the souls, as it would lay open the
genesis of all institutions, customs and manners.
The book had been grand if the Hebraism had
been omitted and the law stated without Gothi-
cism, as ethics, and with that scope for ascension
of state which the nature of things requires. It
is a fine Platonic development of the science of
marriage; teaching that sex is universal, and
not local; virility in the male qualifying every
organ, act, and thought; and the feminine in

woman. Therefore in the real or spiritual world the nuptial union is not momentary, but incessant and total; and chastity not a local, but a universal virtue; unchastity being discovered as much in the trading, or planting, or speaking, or philosophizing, as in generation; and that, though the virgins he saw in heaven were beautiful, the wives were incomparably more beautiful, and went on increasing in beauty evermore.

Yet Swedenborg, after his mode, pinned his theory to a temporary form. He exaggerates the circumstance of marriage; and though he finds false marriages on earth, fancies a wiser choice in heaven. But of progressive souls, all loves and friendships are momentary. *Do you love me?* means, Do you see the same truth? If you do, we are happy with the same happiness: but presently one of us passes into the perception of new truth; — we are divorced, and no tension in nature can hold us to each other. I know how delicious is this cup of love,— I existing for you, you existing for me; but it is a child's clinging to his toy; an attempt to eternize the fireside and nuptial chamber; to keep the picture-alphabet through which our first lessons are prettily conveyed. The Eden of God is bare and grand: like the out-door landscape remembered from the evening fire-side, it seems cold and desolate whilst you cower

over the coals, but once abroad again, we pity
those who can forego the magnificence of nature
for candle-light and cards.   Perhaps the true
subject of the " Conjugal Love " is *Conversation,*
whose laws are profoundly set forth.   It is false,
if literally applied to marriage.   For God is the
bride or bridegroom of the soul.   Heaven is not
the pairing of two, but the communion of all souls.
We meet, and dwell an instant under the temple
of one thought, and part, as though we parted
not, to join another thought in other fellowships
of joy.   So far from there being anything divine
in the low and proprietary sense of *Do you love
me ?* it is only when you leave and lose me by
casting yourself on a sentiment which is higher
than both of us, that I draw near and find myself
at your side ; and I am repelled if you fix your
eye on me and demand love.   In fact, in the spiritual world we change sexes every moment.   You
love the worth in me ; then I am your husband :
but it is not me, but the worth, that fixes the
love ; and that worth is a drop of the ocean of
worth that is beyond me.   Meantime I adore the
greater worth in another, and so become his wife.
He aspires to a higher worth in another spirit,
and is wife or receiver of that influence.

Whether from a self-inquisitorial habit that he

grew into from jealousy of the sins to which men
of thought are liable, he has acquired, in disentan-
gling and demonstrating that particular form of
moral disease, an acumen which no conscience can
resist. I refer to his feeling of the profanation of
thinking to what is good, " from scientifics." " To
reason about faith, is to doubt and deny." He
was painfully alive to the difference between knowing and doing, and this sensibility is incessantly
expressed. Philosophers are, therefore, vipers,
cockatrices, asps, hemorrhoids, presters, and flying
serpents; literary men are conjurors and charla-
tans.

But this topic suggests a sad afterthought, that
here we find the seat of his own pain. Possibly
Swedenborg paid the penalty of introverted faculties. Success, or a fortunate genius, seems to
depend on a happy adjustment of heart and brain ;
on a due proportion, hard to hit, of moral and
mental power, which perhaps obeys the law of
those chemical ratios which make a proportion in
volumes necessary to combination, as when gases
will combine in certain fixed rates, but not at any
rate. It is hard to carry a full cup ; and this man,
profusely endowed in heart and mind, early fell
into dangerous discord with himself. In his Animal Kingdom he surprised us by declaring that he
loved analysis, and not synthesis ; and now, after

his fiftieth year, he falls into jealousy of his intellect; and though aware that truth is not solitary
nor is goodness solitary, but both must ever mix
and marry, he makes war on his mind, takes the
part of the conscience against it, and, on all occasions, traduces and blasphemes it. The violence
is instantly avenged. Beauty is disgraced, love
is unlovely, when truth, the half part of heaven,
is denied, as much as when a bitterness in men
of talent leads to satire and destroys the judgment.
He is wise, but wise in his own despite. There is
an air of infinite grief and the sound of wailing all
over and through this lurid universe. A vampyre
sits in the seat of the prophet and turns with
gloomy appetite to the images of pain. Indeed, a
bird does not more readily weave its nest, or a
mole bore into the ground, than this seer of the
souls substructs a new hell and pit, each more
abominable than the last, round every new crew
of offenders. He was let down through a column
that seemed of brass, but it was formed of angelic
spirits, that he might descend safely amongst the
unhappy, and witness the vastation of souls and
hear there, for a long continuance, their lamenta-
tions: he saw their tormentors, who increase and
strain pangs to infinity; he saw the hell of the
jugglers, the hell of the assassins, the hell of the
lascivious; the hell of robbers, who kill and boil

men; the infernal tun of the deceitful; the excre-
mentitious hells; the hell of the revengeful, whose
faces resembled a round, broad cake, and their
arms rotate like a wheel. Except Rabelais and
Dean Swift nobody ever had such science of filth
and corruption.

These books should be used with caution. It is
dangerous to sculpture these evanescing images of
thought. True in transition, they become false if
fixed. It requires, for his just apprehension, almost a genius equal to his own. But when his
visions become the stereotyped language of multitudes of persons of all degrees of age and capacity,
they are perverted. The wise people of the Greek
race were accustomed to lead the most intelligent
and virtuous young men, as part of their education,
through the Eleusinian mysteries, wherein, with
much pomp and graduation, the highest truths
known to ancient wisdom were taught. An ardent and contemplative young man, at eighteen or
twenty years, might read once these books of
Swedenborg, these mysteries of love and conscience,
and then throw them aside for ever. Genius is
ever haunted by similar dreams, when the hells
and the heavens are opened to it. But these pictures are to be held as mystical, that is, as a quite
arbitrary and accidental picture of the truth, — not
as the truth. Any other symbol would be as good;
then this is safely seen.

Swedenborg's system of the world wants central spontaneity; it is dynamic, not vital, and lacks power to generate life. There is no individual in it. The universe is a gigantic crystal, all whose atoms and laminæ lie in uninterrupted order and with unbroken unity, but cold and still. What seems an individual and a will, is none. There is an immense chain of intermediation, extending from centre to extremes, which bereaves every agency of all freedom and character. The universe, in his poem, suffers under a magnetic sleep, and only reflects the mind of the magnetizer. Every thought comes into each mind by influence from a society of spirits that surround it, and into these from a higher society, and so on. All his types mean the same few things. All his figures speak one speech. All his interlocutors Swedenborgize. Be they who they may, to this complexion must they come at last. This Charon ferries them all over in his boat; kings, counsellors, cavaliers, doctors, Sir Isaac Newton, Sir Hans Sloane, King George II., Mahomet, or whomsoever, and all gather one grimness of hue and style. Only when Cicero comes by, our gentle seer sticks a little at saying he talked with Cicero, and with a touch of human relenting remarks, " one whom it was given me to believe was Cicero " ; and when the *soi disant* Roman opens his mouth, Rome and eloquence have ebbed away, — it is plain

theologic Swedenborg like the rest. His heavens
and hells are dull; fault of want of individualism.
The thousand - fold relation of men is not there.
The interest that attaches in nature to each man,
because he is right by his wrong, and wrong by his
right; because he defies all dogmatizing and classi-
fication, so many allowances and contingences and
futurities are to be taken into account; strong by
his vices, often paralyzed by his virtues; — sinks
into entire sympathy with his society. This want
reacts to the centre of the system. Though the
agency of "the Lord" is in every line referred to
by name, it never becomes alive. There is no lustre
in that eye which gazes from the centre and which
should vivify the immense dependency of beings.

The vice of Swedenborg's mind is its theologic
determination. Nothing with him has the liberality of universal wisdom, but we are always in a
church. That Hebrew muse, which taught the lore
of right and wrong to men, had the same excess of
influence for him it has had for the nations. The
mode, as well as the essence, was sacred. Palestine
is ever the more valuable as a chapter in universal
history, and ever the less an available element in
education. The genius of Swedenborg, largest of
all modern souls in this department of thought,
wasted itself in the endeavor to reanimate and con-
serve what had already arrived at its natural term,

and, in the great secular Providence, was retiring from its prominence, before Western modes of thought and expression. Swedenborg and Behmen both failed by attaching themselves to the Christian symbol, instead of to the moral sentiment, which carries innumerable christianities, humanities, divinities, in its bosom.

The excess of influence shows itself in the incongruous importation of a foreign rhetoric. ' What have I to do ' asks the impatient reader, ' with jasper and sardonyx, beryl and chalcedony; what with arks and passovers, ephahs and ephods; what with lepers and emerods; what with heave-offerings and unleavened bread, chariots of fire, dragons crowned and horned, behemoth and unicorn? Good for Orientals, these are nothing to me. The more learning you bring to explain them, the more glaring the impertinence. The more coherent and elaborate the system, the less I like it. I say, with the Spartan, " Why do you speak so much to the purpose, of that which is nothing to the purpose?" My learning is such as God gave me in my birth and habit, in the delight and study of my eyes and not of another man's. Of all absurdities, this of some foreigner proposing to take away my rhetoric and substitute his own, and amuse me with pelican and stork, instead of thrush and robin; palm-trees and shittim - wood, instead of sassafras and hickory, — seems the most needless.'

Locke said, " God, when he makes the prophet, does not unmake the man." Swedenborg's history points the remark. The parish disputes in the Swedish church between the friends and foes of Luther and Melancthon, concerning " faith alone " and " works alone," intrude themselves into his speculations upon the economy of the universe, and of the celestial societies. The Lutheran bishop's son, for whom the heavens are opened, so that he sees with eyes and in the richest symbolic forms the awful truth of things, and utters again in his books, as under a heavenly mandate, the indisputable secrets of moral nature, — with all these grandeurs resting upon him, remains the Lutheran bishop's son; his judgments are those of a Swedish polemic, and his vast enlargements purchased by adamantine limitations. He carries his controversial memory with him in his visits to the souls. He is like Michael Angelo, who, in his frescoes, put the cardinal who had offended him to roast under a mountain of devils; or like Dante, who avenged, in vindictive melodies, all his private wrongs; or perhaps still more like Montaigne's parish priest, who, if a hail-storm passes over the village, thinks the day of doom is come, and the cannibals already have got the pip. Swedenborg confounds us not less with the pains of Melancthon and Luther and Wolfius, and his own books, which he advertises among the angels.

Under the same theologic cramp, many of his dogmas are bound. His cardinal position in morals is that evils should be shunned as sins. But he does not know what evil is, or what good is, who thinks any ground remains to be occupied, after saying that evil is to be shunned as evil. I doubt not he was led by the desire to insert the element of personality of Deity. But nothing is added. One man, you say, dreads erysipelas, — show him that this dread is evil: or, one dreads hell, — show him that *dread* is evil. He who loves goodness, harbors angels, reveres reverence and lives with God. The less we have to do with our sins the better. No man can afford to waste his moments in compunctions. "That is active duty," say the Hindoos, "which is not for our bondage; that is knowledge, which is for our liberation: all other duty is good only unto weariness."

Another dogma, growing out of this pernicious theologic limitation, is his Inferno. Swedenborg has devils. Evil, according to old philosophers, is good in the making. That pure malignity can exist is the extreme proposition of unbelief. It is not to be entertained by a rational agent; it is atheism; it is the last profanation. Euripides rightly said, —

> "Goodness and being in the gods are one;
> He who imputes ill to them makes them none."

To what a painful perversion had Gothic theology arrived, that Swedenborg admitted no conversion for evil spirits! But the divine effort is never relaxed; the carrion in the sun will convert itself to grass and flowers; and man, though in brothels, or jails, or on gibbets, is on his way to all that is good and true. Burns, with the wild humor of his apostrophe to poor "auld Nickie Ben,"

"O wad ye tak a thought, and mend!"

has the advantage of the vindictive theologian. Every thing is superficial and perishes but love and truth only. The largest is always the truest sentiment, and we feel the more generous spirit of the Indian Vishnu, — "I am the same to all mankind. There is not one who is worthy of my love or hatred. They who serve me with adoration, — I am in them, and they in me. If one whose ways are altogether evil serve me alone, he is as respectable as the just man; he is altogether well employed; he soon becometh of a virtuous spirit and obtaineth eternal happiness."

For the anomalous pretension of Revelations of the other world, — only his probity and genius can entitle it to any serious regard. His revelations destroy their credit by running into detail. If a man say that the Holy Ghost has informed him that the Last Judgment (or the last of the

judgments), took place in 1757; or that the
Dutch, in the other world, live in a heaven by
themselves, and the English in a heaven by themselves; I reply that the Spirit which is holy is
reserved, taciturn, and deals in laws. The rumors
of ghosts and hobgoblins gossip and tell fortunes.
The teachings of the high Spirit are abstemious,
and, in regard to particulars, negative. Socrates's
Genius did not advise him to act or to find, but if
he purposed to do somewhat not advantageous, it
dissuaded him. "What God is," he said, "I know
not; what he is not, I know." The Hindoos have
denominated the Supreme Being, the "Internal
Check." The illuminated Quakers explained their
Light, not as somewhat which leads to any action,
but it appears as an obstruction to any thing unfit.
But the right examples are private experiences,
which are absolutely at one on this point. Strictly
speaking, Swedenborg's revelation is a confounding
of planes, — a capital offence in so learned a cate-
gorist. This is to carry the law of surface into
the plane of substance, to carry individualism and
its fopperies into the realm of essences and generals, — which is dislocation and chaos.

The secret of heaven is kept from age to age.
No imprudent, no sociable angel ever dropt an
early syllable to answer the longings of saints, the
fears of mortals. We should have listened on our

knees to any favorite, who, by stricter obedience,
had brought his thoughts into parallelism with the
celestial currents and could hint to human ears the
scenery and circumstance of the newly parted soul.
But it is certain that it must tally with what is best
in nature. It must not be inferior in tone to the
already known works of the artist who sculptures
the globes of the firmament and writes the moral
law. It must be fresher than rainbows, stabler
than mountains, agreeing with flowers, with tides
and the rising and setting of autumnal stars.
Melodious poets shall be hoarse as street ballads
when once the penetrating key-note of nature and
spirit is sounded, — the earth-beat, sea-beat, heart-
beat, which makes the tune to which the sun rolls,
and the globule of blood, and the sap of trees.

In this mood we hear the rumor that the seer
has arrived, and his tale is told. But there is no
beauty, no heaven : for angels, goblins. The sad
muse loves night and death and the pit. His Inferno is mesmeric. His spiritual world bears the
same relation to the generosities and joys of truth
of which human souls have already made us cognizant, as a man's bad dreams bear to his ideal life.
It is indeed very like, in its endless power of lurid
pictures, to the phenomena of dreaming, which
nightly turns many an honest gentleman, benevo-
lent but dyspeptic, into a wretch, skulking like a

dog about the outer yards and kennels of creation.
When he mounts into the heaven, I do not hear
its language. A man should not tell me that he
has walked among the angels; his proof is that his
eloquence makes me one. Shall the archangels be
less majestic and sweet than the figures that have
actually walked the earth? These angels that
Swedenborg paints give us no very high idea of
their discipline and culture: they are all country
parsons: their heaven is a *fête champêtre*, an
evangelical picnic, or French distribution of prizes
to virtuous peasants. Strange, scholastic, didactic,
passionless, bloodless man, who denotes classes of
souls as a botanist disposes of a carex, and visits
doleful hells as a stratum of chalk or hornblende!
He has no sympathy. He goes up and down the
world of men, a modern Rhadamanthus in gold-
headed cane and peruke, and with nonchalance
and the air of a referee, distributes souls. The
warm, many-weathered, passionate-peopled world
is to him a grammar of hieroglyphs, or an emblematic freemason's procession. How different is
Jacob Behmen! *he* is tremulous with emotion and
listens awe-struck, with the gentlest humanity, to
the Teacher whose lessons he conveys; and when
he asserts that, " in some sort, love is greater than
God," his heart beats so high that the thumping
against his leathern coat is audible across the cen-

turies. 'T is a great difference. Behmen is health-
ily and beautifully wise, notwithstanding the mystical narrowness and incommunicableness. Swedenborg is disagreeably wise, and with all his accumulated gifts, paralyzes and repels.

It is the best sign of a great nature that it opens
a foreground, and, like the breath of morning
landscapes, invites us onward. Swedenborg is retrospective, nor can we divest him of his mattock
and shroud. Some minds are for ever restrained
from descending into nature; others are for ever
prevented from ascending out of it. With a force
of many men, he could never break the umbilical
cord which held him to nature, and he did not rise
to the platform of pure genius.

It is remarkable that this man, who, by his perception of symbols, saw the poetic construction of
things and the primary relation of mind to matter,
remained entirely devoid of the whole apparatus of
poetic expression, which that perception creates.
He knew the grammar and rudiments of the
Mother-Tongue, — how could he not read off one
strain into music? Was he like Saadi, who, in
his vision, designed to fill his lap with the celestial
flowers, as presents for his friends; but the fra-
grance of the roses so intoxicated him that the
skirt dropped from his hands? or is reporting a
breach of the manners of that heavenly society?

or was it that he saw the vision intellectually, and hence that chiding of the intellectual that pervades his books? Be it as it may, his books have no melody, no emotion, no humor, no relief to the dead prosaic level. In his profuse and accurate imagery is no pleasure, for there is no beauty. We wander forlorn in a lack-lustre landscape. No bird ever sang in all these gardens of the dead. The entire want of poetry in so transcendent a mind betokens the disease, and like a hoarse voice in a beautiful person, is a kind of warning. I think, sometimes, he will not be read longer. His great name will turn a sentence. His books have become a monument. His laurel so largely mixed with cypress, a charnel-breath so mingles with the temple incense, that boys and maids will shun the spot.

Yet in this immolation of genius and fame at the shrine of conscience, is a merit sublime beyond praise. He lived to purpose: he gave a verdict. He elected goodness as the clue to which the soul must cling in all this labyrinth of nature. Many opinions conflict as to the true centre. In the shipwreck, some cling to running rigging, some to cask and barrel, some to spars, some to mast; the pilot chooses with science, — I plant myself here; all will sink before this; " he comes to land who sails with me." Do not rely on heavenly favor, or on compassion to folly, or on prudence, on common sense, the old usage and main chance of men : nothing can keep you, — not fate, nor health, nor admirable intellect ; none can keep you, but rectitude only, rectitude for ever and ever ! And with a tenacity that never swerved in all his studies, inventions, dreams, he adheres to this brave choice. I think of him as of some transmigrating votary of Indian legend, who says ' Though I be dog, or jackal, or pismire, in the last rudiments of nature, under what integument or ferocity, I cleave to right, as the sure ladder that leads up to man and to God.'

Swedenborg has rendered a double service to mankind, which is now only beginning to be known. By the science of experiment and use, he made his first steps : he observed and published the laws of nature ; and ascending by just degrees from events to their summits and causes, he was fired with piety at the harmonies he felt, and abandoned himself to his joy and worship. This was his first service. If the glory was too bright for his eyes to bear, if he staggered under the trance of delight, the more excellent is the spectacle he saw, the realities of being which beam and blaze through him, and which no infirmities of the prophet are suffered to obscure ; and he renders a second passive service to men, not less than the first, perhaps, in the great circle of being, — and, in the retributions of spiritual nature, not less glorious or less beautiful to himself.

MONTAIGNE; OR, THE SKEPTIC.

IV.

MONTAIGNE; OR, THE SKEPTIC.

———————

EVERY fact is related on one side to sensation, and on the other to morals. The game of thought is, on the appearance of one of these two sides, to find the other: given the upper, to find the under side. Nothing so thin but has these two faces, and when the observer has seen the obverse, he turns it over to see the reverse. Life is a pitching of this penny, — heads or tails. We never tire of this game, because there is still a slight shudder of astonishment at the exhibition of the other face, at the contrast of the two faces. A man is flushed with success, and bethinks himself what this good luck signifies. He drives his bargain in the street; but it occurs that he also is bought and sold. He sees the beauty of a human face, and searches the cause of that beauty, which must be more beautiful. He builds his fortunes, maintains the laws, cherishes his children; but he asks himself, Why? and whereto? This head and this tail are called, in the language of philosophy, Infinite and Finite;

Relative and Absolute; Apparent and Real; and many fine names beside.

Each man is born with a predisposition to one or the other of these sides of nature; and it will easily happen that men will be found devoted to one or the other. One class has the perception of difference, and is conversant with facts and surfaces, cities and persons, and the bringing certain things to pass; — the men of talent and action. Another class have the perception of identity, and are men of faith and philosophy, men of genius.

Each of these riders drives too fast. Plotinus believes only in philosophers; Fenelon, in saints; Pindar and Byron, in poets. Read the haughty language in which Plato and the Platonists speak of all men who are not devoted to their own shining abstractions: other men are rats and mice. The literary class is usually proud and exclusive. The correspondence of Pope and Swift describes mankind around them as monsters; and that of Goethe and Schiller, in our own time, is scarcely more kind.

It is easy to see how this arrogance comes. The genius is a genius by the first look he casts on any object. Is his eye creative? Does he not rest in angles and colors, but beholds the design? — he will presently undervalue the actual object. In powerful moments, his thought has dissolved the works of art and nature into their causes, so that the works appear heavy and faulty. He has a conception of beauty which the sculptor cannot embody. Picture, statue, temple, railroad, steam-engine, existed first in an artist's mind, without flaw, mistake, or friction, which impair the executed models. So did the Church, the State, college, court, social circle, and all the institutions. It is not strange that these men, remembering what they have seen and hoped of ideas, should affirm disdainfully the superiority of ideas. Having at some time seen that the happy soul will carry all the arts in power, they say, Why cumber ourselves with superfluous realizations? and like dreaming beggars they assume to speak and act as if these values were already substantiated.

On the other part, the men of toil and trade and luxury, — the animal world, including the animal in the philosopher and poet also, and the practical world, including the painful drudgeries which are never excused to philosopher or poet any more than to the rest, — weigh heavily on the other side. The trade in our streets believes in no metaphysical causes, thinks nothing of the force which necessitated traders and a trading planet to exist: no, but sticks to cotton, sugar, wool and salt. The ward meetings, on election days, are not softened by any misgiving of the

value of these ballotings. Hot life is streaming
in a single direction. To the men of this world,
to the animal strength and spirits, to the men of
practical power, whilst immersed in it, the man
of ideas appears out of his reason. They alone
have reason.

Things always bring their own philosophy with
them, that is, prudence. No man acquires property without acquiring with it a little arithmetic
also. In England, the richest country that ever
existed, property stands for more, compared with
personal ability, than in any other. After dinner,
a man believes less, denies more : verities have
lost some charm. After dinner, arithmetic is the
only science : ideas are disturbing, incendiary,
follies of young men, repudiated by the solid portion of society : and a man comes to be valued
by his athletic and animal qualities. Spence relates that Mr. Pope was with Sir Godfrey Kneller
one day, when his nephew, a Guinea trader, came
in. "Nephew," said Sir Godfrey, "you have the
honor of seeing the two greatest men in the
world." "I don't know how great men you may
be," said the Guinea man, "but I don't like your
looks. I have often bought a man much better
than both of you, all muscles and bones, for ten
guineas." Thus the men of the senses revenge
themselves on the professors and repay scorn for

scorn. The first had leaped to conclusions not yet ripe, and say more than is true; the others make themselves merry with the philosopher, and weigh man by the pound. They believe that mustard bites the tongue, that pepper is hot, friction-matches incendiary, revolvers are to be avoided, and suspenders hold up pantaloons; that there is much sentiment in a chest of tea; and a man will be eloquent, if you give him good wine. Are you tender and scrupulous, — you must eat more mince-pie. They hold that Luther had milk in him when he said, —

> "Wer nicht liebt Wein, Weiber, Gesang,
> Der bleibt ein Narr sein Leben lang;" —

and when he advised a young scholar, perplexed with fore-ordination and free-will, to get well drunk. "The nerves," says Cabanis, "they are the man." My neighbor, a jolly farmer, in the tavern bar-room, thinks that the use of money is sure and speedy spending. For his part, he says, he puts his down his neck and gets the good of it.

The inconvenience of this way of thinking is that it runs into indifferentism and then into disgust. Life is eating us up. We shall be fables presently. Keep cool: it will be all one a hundred years hence. Life's well enough, but we shall be glad to get out of it, and they will all be glad to have us. Why should we fret and drudge? Our meat will taste to-morrow as it did yesterday, and we may at last have had enough of it. "Ah," said my languid gentleman at Oxford, "there's nothing new or true,—and no matter."

With a little more bitterness, the cynic moans; our life is like an ass led to market by a bundle of hay being carried before him; he sees nothing but the bundle of hay. "There is so much trouble in coming into the world," said Lord Bolingbroke, "and so much more, as well as meanness, in going out of it, that 't is hardly worth while to be here at all." I knew a philosopher of this kidney who was accustomed briefly to sum up his experience of human nature in saying, "Mankind is a damned rascal:" and the natural corollary is pretty sure to follow, — 'The world lives by humbug, and so will I.'

The abstractionist and the materialist thus mutually exasperating each other, and the scoffer expressing the worst of materialism, there arises a third party to occupy the middle ground between these two, the skeptic, namely. He finds both wrong by being in extremes. He labors to plant his feet, to be the beam of the balance. He will not go beyond his card. He sees the one-sidedness of these men of the street; he will not be a Gibeonite; he stands for the intellectual faculties, a cool head and whatever serves to keep it cool; no unadvised industry, no unrewarded self-devotion, no loss of the brains in toil. Am I an ox, or a dray? — You are both in extremes, he says. You that will have all solid, and a world of pig-lead, deceive yourselves grossly. You believe yourselves rooted and grounded on adamant; and yet, if we uncover the last facts of our knowledge, you are spinning like bubbles in a river, you know not whither or whence, and you are bottomed and capped and wrapped in delusions. Neither will he be betrayed to a book and wrapped in a gown. The studious class are their own victims; they are thin and pale, their feet are cold, their heads are hot, the night is without sleep, the day a fear of interruption, — pallor, squalor, hunger and egotism. If you come near them and see what conceits they entertain, — they are abstractionists, and spend their days and nights in dreaming some dream; in expecting the homage of society to some precious scheme, built on a truth, but destitute of proportion in its presentment, of justness in its application, and of all energy of will in the schemer to embody and vitalize it.

But I see plainly, he says, that I cannot see. I know that human strength is not in extremes, but in avoiding extremes. I, at least, will shun the weakness of philosophizing beyond my depth.

What is the use of pretending to powers we have
not? What is the use of pretending to assurances
we have not, respecting the other life? Why exaggerate the power of virtue? Why be an angel
before your time? These strings, wound up too
high, will snap. If there is a wish for immortality,
and no evidence, why not say just that? If there
are conflicting evidences, why not state them? If
there is not ground for a candid thinker to make
up his mind, yea or nay, — why not suspend the
judgment? I weary of these dogmatizers. I tire
of these hacks of routine, who deny the dogmas.
I neither affirm nor deny. I stand here to try the
case. I am here to consider, σκοπεῖν, to consider
how it is. I will try to keep the balance true. Of
what use to take the chair and glibly rattle off
theories of society, religion and nature, when I
know that practical objections lie in the way, in-
surmountable by me and by my mates? Why so
talkative in public, when each of my neighbors can
pin me to my seat by arguments I cannot refute?
Why pretend that life is so simple a game, when
we know how subtle and elusive the Proteus is?
Why think to shut up all things in your narrow
coop, when we know there are not one or two only,
but ten, twenty, a thousand things, and unlike?
Why fancy that you have all the truth in your
keeping? There is much to say on all sides.

Who shall forbid a wise skepticism, seeing that there is no practical question on which any thing more than an approximate solution can be had? Is not marriage an open question, when it is alleged, from the beginning of the world, that such as are in the institution wish to get out, and such as are out wish to get in? And the reply of Socrates, to him who asked whether he should choose a wife, still remains reasonable, that " whether he should choose one or not, he would repent it." Is not the State a question? All society is divided in opinion on the subject of the State. Nobody loves it; great numbers dislike it and suffer conscientious scruples to allegiance; and the only defence set up, is the fear of doing worse in disorganizing. Is it otherwise with the Church? Or, to put any of the questions which touch mankind nearest, — shall the young man aim at a leading part in law, in politics, in trade? It will not be pretended that a success in either of these kinds is quite coincident with what is best and inmost in his mind. Shall he then, cutting the stays that hold him fast to the social state, put out to sea with no guidance but his genius? There is much to say on both sides. Remember the open question between the present order of " competition " and the friends of " attractive and associated labor." The generous minds embrace the proposition of labor shared

by all ; it is the only honesty; nothing else is safe.
It is from the poor man's hut alone that strength
and virtue come : and yet, on the other side, it is
alleged that labor impairs the form and breaks the
spirit of man, and the laborers cry unanimously,
'We have no thoughts.'   Culture, how indispensable!   I cannot forgive you the want of accomplishments ; and yet culture will instantly impair
that chiefest beauty of spontaneousness.   Excellent
is culture for a savage ; but once let him read in
the book, and he is no longer able not to think of
Plutarch's heroes.   In short, since true fortitude
of understanding consists " in not letting what we
know be embarrassed by what we do not know,"
we ought to secure those advantages which we can
command, and not risk them by clutching after the
airy and unattainable.   Come, no chimeras !   Let
us go abroad ; let us mix in affairs ; let us learn
and get and have and climb.   " Men are a sort of
moving plants, and, like trees, receive a great part
of their nourishment from the air.   If they keep
too much at home, they pine."   Let us have a
robust, manly life ; let us know what we know, for
certain ; what we have, let it be solid and season-
able and our own.   A world in the hand is worth
two in the bush.   Let us have to do with real men
and women, and not with skipping ghosts.

This then is the right ground of the skeptic, —

this of consideration, of self-containing; not at all of unbelief; not at all of universal denying, nor of universal doubting, — doubting even that he doubts; least of all of scoffing and profligate jeering at all that is stable and good. These are no more his moods than are those of religion and philosophy. He is the considerer, the prudent, taking in sail, counting stock, husbanding his means, believing that a man has too many enemies than that he can afford to be his own foe; that we cannot give ourselves too many advantages in this unequal conflict, with powers so vast and unweariable ranged on one side, and this little conceited vulnerable popinjay that a man is, bobbing up and down into every danger, on the other. It is a position taken up for better defence, as of more safety, and one that can be maintained; and it is one of more opportunity and range: as, when we build a house, the rule is to set it not too high nor too low, under the wind, but out of the dirt.

The philosophy we want is one of fluxions and mobility. The Spartan and Stoic schemes are too stark and stiff for our occasion. A theory of Saint John, and of nonresistance, seems, on the other hand, too thin and aerial. We want some coat woven of elastic steel, stout as the first and limber as the second. We want a ship in these billows we inhabit. An angular, dogmatic house would

be rent to chips and splinters in this storm of many
elements. No, it must be tight, and fit to the form
of man, to live at all; as a shell must dictate the
architecture of a house founded on the sea. The
soul of man must be the type of our scheme, just
as the body of man is the type after which a
dwelling-house is built. Adaptiveness is the peculiarity of human nature. We are golden averages,
volitant stabilities, compensated or periodic errors,
houses founded on the sea. The wise skeptic
wishes to have a near view of the best game and
the chief players; what is best in the planet; art
and nature, places and events; but mainly men.
Every thing that is excellent in mankind, — a form
of grace, an arm of iron, lips of persuasion, a brain
of resources, every one skilful to play and win, —
he will see and judge.

The terms of admission to this spectacle are,
that he have a certain solid and intelligible way of
living of his own; some method of answering the
inevitable needs of human life; proof that he has
played with skill and success; that he has evinced
the temper, stoutness and the range of qualities
which, among his contemporaries and countrymen,
entitle him to fellowship and trust. For the secrets
of life are not shown except to sympathy and likeness. Men do not confide themselves to boys, or
coxcombs, or pedants, but to their peers. Some

wise limitation, as the modern phrase is; some condition between the extremes, and having, itself, a positive quality; some stark and sufficient man, who is not salt or sugar, but sufficiently related to the world to do justice to Paris or London, and, at the same time, a vigorous and original thinker, whom cities can not overawe, but who uses them, — is the fit person to occupy this ground of speculation.

These qualities meet in the character of Montaigne. And yet, since the personal regard which I entertain for Montaigne may be unduly great, I will, under the shield of this prince of egotists, offer, as an apology for electing him as the representative of skepticism, a word or two to explain how my love began and grew for this admirable gossip.

A single odd volume of Cotton's translation of the Essays remained to me from my father's library, when a boy. It lay long neglected, until, after many years, when I was newly escaped from college, I read the book, and procured the remaining volumes. I remember the delight and wonder in which I lived with it. It seemed to me as if I had myself written the book, in some former life, so sincerely it spoke to my thought and experience. It happened, when in Paris, in 1833, that, in the cemetery of Père Lachaise, I came to a tomb of Auguste Collignon, who died in 1830, aged sixty-

eight years, and who, said the monument, "lived
to do right, and had formed himself to virtue on
the Essays of Montaigne." Some years later, I
became acquainted with an accomplished English
poet, John Sterling; and, in prosecuting my correspondence, I found that, from a love of Montaigne, he had made a pilgrimage to his chateau,
still standing near Castellan, in Perigord, and, after two hundred and fifty years, had copied from
the walls of his library the inscriptions which Montaigne had written there. That Journal of Mr.
Sterling's, published in the Westminster Review,
Mr. Hazlitt has reprinted in the *Prolegomena* to
his edition of the Essays. I heard with pleasure
that one of the newly-discovered autographs of
William Shakspeare was in a copy of Florio's translation of Montaigne. It is the only book which we
certainly know to have been in the poet's library.
And, oddly enough, the duplicate copy of Florio,
which the British Museum purchased with a view
of protecting the Shakspeare autograph, (as I was
informed in the Museum,) turned out to have the
autograph of Ben Jonson in the fly-leaf. Leigh
Hunt relates of Lord Byron, that Montaigne was
the only great writer of past times whom he read
with avowed satisfaction. Other coincidences, not
needful to be mentioned here, concurred to make
this old Gascon still new and immortal for me.

In 1571, on the death of his father, Montaigne, then thirty-eight years old, retired from the practice of law at Bordeaux, and settled himself on his estate. Though he had been a man of pleasure and sometimes a courtier, his studious habits now grew on him, and he loved the compass, staidness and independence of the country gentleman's life. He took up his economy in good earnest, and made his farms yield the most. Downright and plain-dealing, and abhorring to be deceived or to deceive, he was esteemed in the country for his sense and probity. In the civil wars of the League, which converted every house into a fort, Montaigne kept his gates open and his house without defence. All parties freely came and went, his courage and honor being universally esteemed. The neighboring lords and gentry brought jewels and papers to him for safe - keeping. Gibbon reckons, in these bigoted times, but two men of liberality in France, — Henry IV. and Montaigne.

Montaigne is the frankest and honestest of all writers. His French freedom runs into grossness; but he has anticipated all censure by the bounty of his own confessions. In his times, books were written to one sex only, and almost all were written in Latin; so that in a humorist a certain nakedness of statement was permitted, which our manners, of a literature addressed equally to both

sexes, do not allow. But though a biblical plain-
ness coupled with a most uncanonical levity may
shut his pages to many sensitive readers, yet the
offence is superficial. He parades it: he makes
the most of it: nobody can think or say worse of
him than he does. He pretends to most of the
vices; and, if there be any virtue in him, he says,
it got in by stealth. There is no man, in his opinion, who has not deserved hanging five or six times;
and he pretends no exception in his own behalf.
"Five or six as ridiculous stories," too, he says,
"can be told of me, as of any man living." But,
with all this really superfluous frankness, the opinion of an invincible probity grows into every reader's mind. "When I the most strictly and relig-
iously confess myself, I find that the best virtue I
have has in it some tincture of vice; and I, who
am as sincere and perfect a lover of virtue of that
stamp as any other whatever, am afraid that Plato,
in his purest virtue, if he had listened and laid his
ear close to himself, would have heard some jarring
sound of human mixture; but faint and remote
and only to be perceived by himself."

Here is an impatience and fastidiousness at color
or pretence of any kind. He has been in courts so
long as to have conceived a furious disgust at appearances; he will indulge himself with a little
cursing and swearing; he will talk with sailors and

gipsies, use flash and street ballads; he has stayed in-doors till he is deadly sick; he will to the open air, though it rain bullets. He has seen too much of gentlemen of the long robe, until he wishes for cannibals ; and is so nervous, by factitious life, that he thinks the more barbarous man is, the better he is. He likes his saddle. You may read theology, and grammar, and metaphysics elsewhere. Whatever you get here shall smack of the earth and of real life, sweet, or smart, or stinging. He makes no hesitation to entertain you with the records of his disease, and his journey to Italy is quite full of that matter. He took and kept this position of equilibrium. Over his name he drew an emblematic pair of scales, and wrote *Que sçais je?* under it. As I look at his effigy opposite the title-page, I seem to hear him say, ' You may play old Poz, if you will; you may rail and exaggerate, — I stand here for truth, and will not, for all the states and churches and revenues and personal reputations of Europe, overstate the dry fact, as I see it; I will rather mumble and prose about what I certainly know, — my house and barns; my father, my wife and my tenants ; my old lean bald pate ; my knives and forks ; what meats I eat and what drinks I prefer, and a hundred straws just as ridiculous, — than I will write, with a fine crow-quill, a fine romance. I like gray days, and autumn and winter weather. I am gray and autumnal myself, and think an undress and old shoes that do not pinch my feet, and old friends who do not constrain me, and plain topics where I do not need to strain myself and pump my brains, the most suitable. Our condition as men is risky and ticklish enough. One cannot be sure of himself and his fortune an hour, but he may be whisked off into some pitiable or ridiculous plight. Why should I vapor and play the philosopher, instead of ballasting, the best I can, this dancing balloon? So, at least, I live within compass, keep myself ready for action, and can shoot the gulf at last with decency. If there be any thing farcical in such a life, the blame is not mine: let it lie at fate's and nature's door.'

The Essays, therefore, are an entertaining soliloquy on every random topic that comes into his head; treating every thing without ceremony, yet with masculine sense. There have been men with deeper insight; but, one would say, never a man with such abundance of thoughts: he is never dull, never insincere, and has the genius to make the reader care for all that he cares for.

The sincerity and marrow of the man reaches to his sentences. I know not anywhere the book that seems less written. It is the language of conversation transferred to a book. Cut these words, and they would bleed; they are vascular and alive. One has the same pleasure in it that he feels in listening to the necessary speech of men about their work, when any unusual circumstance gives momentary importance to the dialogue. For blacksmiths and teamsters do not trip in their speech; it is a shower of bullets. It is Cambridge men who correct themselves and begin again at every half sentence, and, moreover, will pun, and refine too much, and swerve from the matter to the expression. Montaigne talks with shrewdness, knows the world and books and himself, and uses the positive degree: never shrieks, or protests, or prays : no weakness, no convulsion, no superlative : does not wish to jump out of his skin, or play any antics, or annihilate space or time, but is stout and solid; tastes every moment of the day; likes pain because it makes him feel himself and realize things; as we pinch ourselves to know that we are awake. He keeps the plain; he rarely mounts or sinks; likes to feel solid ground and the stones underneath. His writing has no enthusiasms, no aspiration; contented, self-respecting and keeping the middle of the road. There is but one exception, — in his love for Socrates. In speaking of him, for once his cheek flushes and his style rises to passion.

Montaigne died of a quinsy, at the age of sixty, in 1592. When he came to die he caused the mass to be celebrated in his chamber. At the age of thirty-three, he had been married. " But," he says, " might I have had my own will, I would not have married Wisdom herself, if she would have had me : but 't is to much purpose to evade it, the common custom and use of life will have it so. Most of my actions are guided by example, not choice." In the hour of death, he gave the same weight to custom. *Que sçais je?* What do I know ?

This book of Montaigne the world has endorsed by translating it into all tongues and printing seventy-five editions of it in Europe ; and that, too, a circulation somewhat chosen, namely among courtiers, soldiers, princes, men of the world and men of wit and generosity.

Shall we say that Montaigne has spoken wisely, and given the right and permanent expression of the human mind, on the conduct of life ?

We are natural believers. Truth, or the connection between cause and effect, alone interests us. We are persuaded that a thread runs through all things : all worlds are strung on it, as beads ; and men, and events, and life, come to us only because of that thread : they pass and repass only that we may know the direction and continuity of that line. A book or statement which goes to show that there is no line, but random and chaos, a calamity out of nothing, a prosperity and no account of it, a hero born from a fool, a fool from a hero, — dispirits us. Seen or unseen, we believe the tie exists. Talent makes counterfeit ties; genius finds the real ones. We hearken to the man of science, because we anticipate the sequence in natural phenomena which he uncovers. We love whatever affirms, connects, preserves ; and dislike what scatters or pulls down. One man appears whose nature is to all men's eyes conserving and constructive : his presence supposes a well-ordered society, agriculture, trade, large institutions and empire. If these did not exist, they would begin to exist through his endeavors. Therefore he cheers and comforts men, who feel all this in him very readily. The nonconformist and the rebel say all manner of unanswerable things against the existing republic, but discover to our sense no plan of house or state of their own. Therefore, though the town and state and way of living, which our counsellor contemplated, might be a very modest or musty prosperity, yet men rightly go for him, and reject the reformer so long as he comes only with axe and crowbar.

But though we are natural conservers and causationists, and reject a sour, dumpish unbelief, the skeptical class, which Montaigne represents, have reason, and every man, at some time, belongs to it.

Every superior mind will pass through this domain of equilibration, — I should rather say, will know how to avail himself of the checks and balances in nature, as a natural weapon against the exaggeration and formalism of bigots and blockheads.

Skepticism is the attitude assumed by the student in relation to the particulars which society adores, but which he sees to be reverend only in their tendency and spirit. The ground occupied by the skeptic is the vestibule of the temple. Society does not like to have any breath of question blown on the existing order. But the interrogation of custom at all points is an inevitable stage in the growth of every superior mind, and is the evidence of its perception of the flowing power which remains itself in all changes.

The superior mind will find itself equally at odds with the evils of society and with the projects that are offered to relieve them. The wise skeptic is a bad citizen; no conservative, he sees the selfishness of property and the drowsiness of institutions. But neither is he fit to work with any democratic party that ever was constituted; for parties wish every one committed, and he penetrates the popular patriotism. His politics are those of the " Soul's Errand " of Sir Walter Raleigh; or of Krishna, in the Bhagavat, " There is none who is worthy of my love or hatred; " whilst he sentences

law, physic, divinity, commerce and custom. He
is a reformer ; yet he is no better member of the
philanthropic association. It turns out that he is
not the champion of the operative, the pauper, the
prisoner, the slave. It stands in his mind that our
life in this world is not of quite so easy interpretation as churches and school-books say. He does
not wish to take ground against these benevolences,
to play the part of devil's attorney, and blazon
every doubt and sneer that darkens the sun for
him. But he says, There are doubts.

I mean to use the occasion, and celebrate the
calendar-day of our Saint Michel de Montaigne, by
counting and describing these doubts or negations.
I wish to ferret them out of their holes and sun
them a little. We must do with them as the police
do with old rogues, who are shown up to the public at the marshal's office. They will never be so
formidable when once they have been identified
and registered. But I mean honestly by them, —
that justice shall be done to their terrors. I shall
not take Sunday objections, made up on purpose to
be put down. I shall take the worst I can find,
whether I can dispose of them or they of me.

I do not press the skepticism of the materialist.
I know the quadruped opinion will not prevail.
'T is of no importance what bats and oxen think.
The first dangerous symptom I report is, the levity

of intellect; as if it were fatal to earnestness to know much. Knowledge is the knowing that we can not know. The dull pray; the geniuses are light mockers. How respectable is earnestness on every platform! but intellect kills it. Nay, San Carlo, my subtle and admirable friend, one of the most penetrating of men, finds that all direct ascension, even of lofty piety, leads to this ghastly insight and sends back the votary orphaned. My astonishing San Carlo thought the lawgivers and saints infected. They found the ark empty; saw, and would not tell; and tried to choke off their approaching followers, by saying, ' Action, action, my dear fellows, is for you!' Bad as was to me this detection by San Carlo, this frost in July, this blow from a bride, there was still a worse, namely the cloy or satiety of the saints. In the mount of vision, ere they have yet risen from their knees, they say, ' We discover that this our homage and beatitude is partial and deformed: we must fly for relief to the suspected and reviled Intellect, to the Understanding, the Mephistopheles, to the gymnastics of talent.'

This is hobgoblin the first; and, though it has been the subject of much elegy in our nineteenth century, from Byron, Goethe and other poets of less fame, not to mention many distinguished private observers, — I confess it is not very affecting to my imagination; for it seems to concern the shattering of baby - houses and crockery - shops. What flutters the Church of Rome, or of England, or of Geneva, or of Boston, may yet be very far from touching any principle of faith. I think that the intellect and moral sentiment are unanimous ; and that though philosophy extirpates bugbears, yet it supplies the natural checks of vice, and polarity to the soul. I think that the wiser a man is, the more stupendous he finds the natural and moral economy, and lifts himself to a more absolute reliance.

There is the power of moods, each setting at nought all but its own tissue of facts and beliefs. There is the power of complexions, obviously modifying the dispositions and sentiments. The beliefs and unbeliefs appear to be structural ; and as soon as each man attains the poise and vivacity which allow the whole machinery to play, he will not need extreme examples, but will rapidly alternate all opinions in his own life. Our life is March weather, savage and serene in one hour. We go forth austere, dedicated, believing in the iron links of Destiny, and will not turn on our heel to save our life : but a book, or a bust, or only the sound of a name, shoots a spark through the nerves, and we suddenly believe in will : my finger-ring shall be the seal of Solomon ; fate is for imbeciles ; all is possible to the resolved mind. Presently a new

experience gives a new turn to our thoughts: common sense resumes its tyranny; we say, ' Well, the
army, after all, is the gate to fame, manners and
poetry: and, look you, — on the whole, selfishness
plants best, prunes best, makes the best commerce
and the best citizen.' Are the opinions of a man
on right and wrong, on fate and causation, at the
mercy of a broken sleep or an indigestion? Is his
belief in God and Duty no deeper than a stomach
evidence? And what guaranty for the permanence
of his opinions? I like not the French celerity, —
a new Church and State once a week. This is
the second negation; and I shall let it pass for
what it will. As far as it asserts rotation of states
of mind, I suppose it suggests its own remedy,
namely in the record of larger periods. What is
the mean of many states; of all the states? Does
the general voice of ages affirm any principle, or is
no community of sentiment discoverable in distant
times and places? And when it shows the power
of self-interest, I accept that as part of the divine
law and must reconcile it with aspiration the best
I can.

The word Fate, or Destiny, expresses the sense
of mankind, in all ages, that the laws of the world
do not always befriend, but often hurt and crush
us. Fate, in the shape of *Kinde* or nature, grows
over us like grass. We paint Time with a scythe;

Love and Fortune, blind ; and Destiny, deaf. We
have too little power of resistance against this ferocity which champs us up. What front can we
make against these unavoidable, victorious, malefi-
cent forces ?   What can I do against the influence
of Race, in my history ?   What can I do against
hereditary and constitutional habits ; against scrof-
ula, lymph, impotence ? against climate, against
barbarism, in my country ?   I can reason down or
deny every thing, except this perpetual Belly : feed
he must and will, and I cannot make him respectable.

But the main resistance which the affirmative
impulse finds, and one including all others, is in
the doctrine of the Illusionists. There is a painful rumor in circulation that we have been prac-
tised upon in all the principal performances of life,
and free agency is the emptiest name. We have
been sopped and drugged with the air, with food,
with woman, with children, with sciences, with
events, which leave us exactly where they found
us. The mathematics, 't is complained, leave the
mind where they find it : so do all sciences ; and so
do all events and actions. I find a man who has
passed through all the sciences, the churl he was ;
and, through all the offices, learned, civil and social, can detect the child. We are not the less

necessitated to dedicate life to them. In fact we may come to accept it as the fixed rule and theory of our state of education, that God is a substance, and his method is illusion. The eastern sages owned the goddess Yoganidra, the great illusory energy of Vishnu, by whom, as utter ignorance, the whole world is beguiled.

Or shall I state it thus? — The astonishment of life is the absence of any appearance of reconciliation between the theory and practice of life. Reason, the prized reality, the Law, is apprehended, now and then, for a serene and profound moment amidst the hubbub of cares and works which have no direct bearing on it ; — is then lost for months or years, and again found for an interval, to be lost again. If we compute it in time, we may, in fifty years, have half a dozen reasonable hours. But what are these cares and works the better? A method in the world we do not see, but this parallelism of great and little, which never react on each other, nor discover the smallest tendency to converge. Experiences, fortunes, governings, readings, writings, are nothing to the purpose ; as when a man comes into the room it does not appear whether he has been fed on yams or buffalo, — he has contrived to get so much bone and fibre as he wants, out of rice or out of snow. So vast is the disproportion between the sky of law and the pismire of performance under it, that whether he is a man of worth or a sot is not so great a matter as we say. Shall I add, as one juggle of this enchantment, the stunning non-intercourse law which makes co-operation impossible? The young spirit pants to enter society. But all the ways of culture and greatness lead to solitary imprisonment. He has been often baulked. He did not expect a sympathy with his thought from the village, but he went with it to the chosen and intelligent, and found no entertainment for it, but mere misapprehension, distaste and scoffing. Men are strangely mistimed and misapplied; and the excellence of each is an inflamed individualism which separates him more.

There are these, and more than these diseases of thought, which our ordinary teachers do not attempt to remove. Now shall we, because a good nature inclines us to virtue's side, say, There are no doubts, — and lie for the right? Is life to be led in a brave or in a cowardly manner? and is not the satisfaction of the doubts essential to all manliness? Is the name of virtue to be a barrier to that which is virtue? Can you not believe that a man of earnest and burly habit may find small good in tea, essays and catechism, and want a rougher instruction, want men, labor, trade, farming, war, hunger, plenty, love, hatred, doubt and

terror to make things plain to him; and has he
not a right to insist on being convinced in his own
way? When he is convinced, he will be worth the
pains.

Belief consists in accepting the affirmations of
the soul; unbelief, in denying them. Some minds
are incapable of skepticism. The doubts they pro-
fess to entertain are rather a civility or accommo-
dation to the common discourse of their company.
They may well give themselves leave to speculate,
for they are secure of a return. Once admitted to
the heaven of thought, they see no relapse into
night, but infinite invitation on the other side.
Heaven is within heaven, and sky over sky, and
they are encompassed with divinities. Others there
are to whom the heaven is brass, and it shuts down
to the surface of the earth. It is a question of
temperament, or of more or less immersion in
nature. The last class must needs have a reflex or
parasite faith; not a sight of realities, but an in-
stinctive reliance on the seers and believers of
realities. The manners and thoughts of believers
astonish them and convince them that these have
seen something which is hid from themselves. But
their sensual habit would fix the believer to his last
position, whilst he as inevitably advances; and presently the unbeliever, for love of belief, burns the
believer.

Great believers are always reckoned infidels, impracticable, fantastic, atheistic, and really men of no account. The spiritualist finds himself driven to express his faith by a series of skepticisms. Charitable souls come with their projects and ask his co-operation. How can he hesitate? It is the rule of mere comity and courtesy to agree where you can, and to turn your sentence with something auspicious, and not freezing and sinister. But he is forced to say, ' O, these things will be as they must be: what can you do? These particular griefs and crimes are the foliage and fruit of such trees as we see growing. It is vain to complain of the leaf or the berry; cut it off, it will bear another just as bad. You must begin your cure lower down.' The generosities of the day prove an intractable element for him. The people's questions are not his; their methods are not his; and against all the dictates of good nature he is driven to say he has no pleasure in them.

Even the doctrines dear to the hope of man, of the divine Providence and of the immortality of the soul, his neighbors can not put the statement so that he shall affirm it. But he denies out of more faith, and not less. He denies out of honesty. He had rather stand charged with the imbecility of skepticism, than with untruth. I believe, he says, in the moral design of the universe; it exists hos-

pitably for the weal of souls; but your dogmas
seem to me caricatures : why should I make believe
them ?   Will any say, This is cold and infidel ?
The wise and magnanimous will not say so.   They
will exult in his far-sighted good-will that can
abandon to the adversary all the ground of tradition and common belief, without losing a jot of
strength.   It sees to the end of all transgression.
George Fox saw that there was "an ocean of darkness and death ; but withal an infinite ocean of
light and love which flowed over that of darkness."

The final solution in which skepticism is lost, is
in the moral sentiment, which never forfeits its
supremacy.   All moods may be safely tried, and
their weight allowed to all objections : the moral
sentiment as easily outweighs them all, as any one.
This is the drop which balances the sea.   I play
with the miscellany of facts, and take those superficial views which we call skepticism ; but I know
that they will presently appear to me in that order
which makes skepticism impossible.   A man of
thought must feel the thought that is parent of
the universe ; that the masses of nature do undu-
late and flow.

This faith avails to the whole emergency of life
and objects.   The world is saturated with deity
and with law.   He is content with just and unjust,

with sots and fools, with the triumph of folly and fraud. He can behold with serenity the yawning gulf between the ambition of man and his power of performance, between the demand and supply of power, which makes the tragedy of all souls.

Charles Fourier announced that " the attractions of man are proportioned to his destinies ; " in other words, that every desire predicts its own satisfaction. Yet all experience exhibits the reverse of this ; the incompetency of power is the universal grief of young and ardent minds. They accuse the divine providence of a certain parsimony. It has shown the heaven and earth to every child and filled him with a desire for the whole ; a desire raging, infinite ; a hunger, as of space to be filled with planets ; a cry of famine, as of devils for souls. Then for the satisfaction, — to each man is administered a single drop, a bead of dew of vital power, *per day*, — a cup as large as space, and one drop of the water of life in it. Each man woke in the morning with an appetite that could eat the solar system like a cake ; a spirit for action and passion without bounds ; he could lay his hand on the morning star ; he could try conclusions with gravitation or chemistry ; but, on the first motion to prove his strength, — hands, feet, senses, gave way and would not serve him. He was an emperor deserted by his states, and left to whistle by him

self, or thrust into a mob of emperors, all whist-
ling: and still the sirens sang, " The attractions are
proportioned to the destinies." In every house,
in the heart of each maiden and of each boy, in the
soul of the soaring saint, this chasm is found, —
between the largest promise of ideal power, and
the shabby experience.

The expansive nature of truth comes to our succor, elastic, not to be surrounded. Man helps himself by larger generalizations. The lesson of life
is practically to generalize; to believe what the
years and the centuries say, against the hours; to
resist the usurpation of particulars; to penetrate
to their catholic sense. Things seem to say one
thing, and say the reverse. The appearance is immoral; the result is moral. Things seem to tend
downward, to justify despondency, to promote
rogues, to defeat the just; and by knaves as by
martyrs the just cause is carried forward. Although knaves win in every political struggle, although society seems to be delivered over from the
hands of one set of criminals into the hands of another set of criminals, as fast as the government
is changed, and the march of civilization is a train
of felonies, — yet, general ends are somehow an-
swered. We see, now, events forced on which
seem to retard or retrograde the civility of ages.
But the world-spirit is a good swimmer, and storms

and waves cannot drown him. He snaps his finger at laws: and so, throughout history, heaven seems to affect low and poor means. Through the years and the centuries, through evil agents, through toys and atoms, a great and beneficent tendency irresistibly streams.

Let a man learn to look for the permanent in the mutable and fleeting; let him learn to bear the disappearance of things he was wont to reverence without losing his reverence; let him learn that he is here, not to work but to be worked upon; and that, though abyss open under abyss, and opinion displace opinion, all are at last contained in the Eternal Cause : —

> " If my bark sink, 't is to another sea."

SHAKSPEARE; OR, THE POET.

V.

SHAKSPEARE; OR, THE POET.

———•———

GREAT men are more distinguished by range
and extent than by originality. If we require the
originality which consists in weaving, like a spider, their web from their own bowels; in finding
clay and making bricks and building the house; no
great men are original. Nor does valuable originality consist in unlikeness to other men. The hero
is in the press of knights and the thick of events;
and seeing what men want and sharing their desire, he adds the needful length of sight and of
arm, to come at the desired point. The greatest
genius is the most indebted man. A poet is no
rattle-brain, saying what comes uppermost, and, because he says every thing, saying at last something
good; but a heart in unison with his time and
country. There is nothing whimsical and fantastic in his production, but sweet and sad earnest,
freighted with the weightiest convictions and pointed with the most determined aim which any man
or class knows of in his times.

The Genius of our life is jealous of individuals, and will not have any individual great, except through the general. There is no choice to genius. [A great man does not wake up on some fine morning and say, ' I am full of life, I will go to sea and find an Antarctic continent : to-day I will square the circle : I will ransack botany and find a new food for man : I have a new architecture in my mind : I foresee a new mechanic power : ' no, but he finds himself in the river of the thoughts and events, forced onward by the ideas and necessities of his contemporaries.] He stands where all the eyes of men look one way, and their hands all point in the direction in which he should go. The Church has reared him amidst rites and pomps, and he carries out the advice which her music gave him, and builds a cathedral needed by her chants and processions. He finds a war raging : it educates him, by trumpet, in barracks, and he betters the instruction. He finds two counties groping to bring coal, or flour, or fish, from the place of production to the place of consumption, and he hits on a railroad. Every master has found his materials collected, and his power lay in his sympathy with his people and in his love of the materials he wrought in. What an economy of power ! and what a compensation for the shortness of life ! All is done to his hand. The world has brought him thus far on his way. The human race has gone out before him, sunk the hills, filled the hollows and bridged the rivers. Men, nations, poets, artisans, women, all have worked for him, and he enters into their labors. Choose any other thing, out of the line of tendency, out of the national feeling and history, and he would have all to do for himself: his powers would be expended in the first preparations. Great genial power, one would almost say, consists in not being original at all; in being altogether receptive ; in letting the world do all, and suffering the spirit of the hour to pass unobstructed through the mind.

Shakspeare's youth fell in a time when the English people were importunate for dramatic entertainments. The court took offence easily at political allusions and attempted to suppress them. The Puritans, a growing and energetic party, and the religious among the Anglican church, would suppress them. But the people wanted them. Inn-yards, houses without roofs, and extemporaneous enclosures at country fairs were the ready theatres of strolling players. The people had tasted this new joy ; and, as we could not hope to suppress newspapers now, — no, not by the strongest party, — neither then could king, prelate, or puritan, alone or united, suppress an organ which was ballad, epic, newspaper, caucus, lecture, Punch and library, at the same time. Probably king, prelate and puritan, all found their own account in it. It had become, by all causes, a national interest, — by no means conspicuous, so that some great scholar would have thought of treating it in an English history, — but not a whit less considerable because it was cheap and of no account, like a baker's-shop. The best proof of its vitality is the crowd of writers which suddenly broke into this field; Kyd, Marlow, Greene, Jonson, Chapman, Dekker, Webster, Heywood, Middleton, Peele, Ford, Massinger, Beaumont and Fletcher.

The secure possession, by the stage, of the public mind, is of the first importance to the poet who works for it. He loses no time in idle experiments. Here is audience and expectation prepared. In the case of Shakspeare there is much more. At the time when he left Stratford and went up to London, a great body of stage-plays of all dates and writers existed in manuscript and were in turn produced on the boards. Here is the Tale of Troy, which the audience will bear hearing some part of, every week; the Death of Julius Cæsar, and other stories out of Plutarch, which they never tire of; a shelf full of English history, from the chronicles of Brut and Arthur, down to the royal Henries, which men hear eagerly; and a string of doleful tragedies, merry Italian tales and Spanish

voyages, which all the London 'prentices know.
All the mass has been treated, with more or less
skill, by every playwright, and the prompter has the
soiled and tattered manuscripts. It is now no
longer possible to say who wrote them first. They
have been the property of the Theatre so long, and
so many rising geniuses have enlarged or altered
them, inserting a speech or a whole scene, or adding a song, that no man can any longer claim copyright in this work of numbers. Happily, no man
wishes to. They are not yet desired in that way.
We have few readers, many spectators and hearers.
They had best lie where they are.

Shakspeare, in common with his comrades, esteemed the mass of old plays waste stock, in which
any experiment could be freely tried. Had the
prestige which hedges about a modern tragedy existed, nothing could have been done. The rude
warm blood of the living England circulated in the
play, as in street-ballads, and gave body which
he wanted to his airy and majestic fancy. The
poet needs a ground in popular tradition on which
he may work, and which, again, may restrain his
art within the due temperance. It holds him to
the people, supplies a foundation for his edifice,
and in furnishing so much work done to his hand,
leaves him at leisure and in full strength for the
audacities of his imagination In short, the poet

owes to his legend what sculpture owed to the temple. Sculpture in Egypt and in Greece grew up
in subordination to architecture.   It was the orna-
ment of the temple wall : at first a rude relief
carved on pediments, then the relief became bolder
and a head or arm was projected from the wall ;
the groups being still arranged with reference to
the building, which serves also as a frame to hold
the figures ; and when at last the greatest freedom
of style and treatment was reached, the prevailing
genius of architecture still enforced a certain calmness and continence in the statue.   As soon as the
statue was begun for itself, and with no reference
to the temple or palace, the art began to decline :
freak, extravagance and exhibition took the place
of the old temperance.   This balance-wheel, which
the sculptor found in architecture, the perilous irri-
tability of poetic talent found in the accumulated
dramatic materials to which the people were already wonted, and which had a certain excellence
which no single genius, however extraordinary,
could hope to create.

In point of fact it appears that Shakspeare did
owe debts in all directions, and was able to use
whatever he found ; and the amount of indebted-
ness may be inferred from Malone's laborious com-
putations in regard to the First, Second and Third
parts of Henry VI., in which, " out of 6,043 lines,

1,771 were written by some author preceding Shakspeare, 2,373 by him, on the foundation laid by his
predecessors, and 1,899 were entirely his own."
And the proceeding investigation hardly leaves a
single drama of his absolute invention. Malone's
sentence is an important piece of external history.
In Henry VIII. I think I see plainly the cropping
out of the original rock on which his own finer
stratum was laid. The first play was written by a
superior, thoughtful man, with a vicious ear. I can
mark his lines, and know well their cadence. See
Wolsey's soliloquy, and the following scene with
Cromwell, where instead of the metre of Shakspeare,
whose secret is that the thought constructs the tune,
so that reading for the sense will best bring out
the rhythm, — here the lines are constructed on a
given tune, and the verse has even a trace of pulpit
eloquence. But the play contains through all its
length unmistakable traits of Shakspeare's hand,
and some passages, as the account of the coronation,
are like autographs. What is odd, the compliment
to Queen Elizabeth is in the bad rhythm.

Shakspeare knew that tradition supplies a better
fable than any invention can. If he lost any credit
of design, he augmented his resources; and, at
that day, our petulant demand for originality was
not so much pressed. There was no literature for
the million. The universal reading, the cheap

press, were unknown. A great poet who appears in illiterate times, absorbs into his sphere all the light which is any where radiating. Every intellectual jewel, every flower of sentiment it is his fine office to bring to his people; and he comes to value his memory equally with his invention. He is therefore little solicitous whence his thoughts have been derived; whether through translation, whether through tradition, whether by travel in distant countries, whether by inspiration; from whatever source, they are equally welcome to his uncritical audience. Nay, he borrows very near home. Other men say wise things as well as he; only they say a good many foolish things, and do not know when they have spoken wisely. He knows the sparkle of the true stone, and puts it in high place, wherever he finds it. Such is the happy position of Homer perhaps; of Chaucer, of Saadi. They felt that all wit was their wit. And they are librarians and historiographers, as well as poëts. Each romancer was heir and dispenser of all the hundred tales of the world, —

> " Presenting Thebes' and Pelops' line
> And the tale of Troy divine."

The influence of Chaucer is conspicuous in all our early literature; and more recently not only Pope and Dryden have been beholden to him, but, in the whole society of English writers, a large unacknowl·

edged debt is easily traced. One is charmed with
the opulence which feeds so many pensioners. But
Chaucer is a huge borrower. Chaucer, it seems,
drew continually, through Lydgate and Caxton,
from Guido di Colonna, whose Latin romance of
the Trojan war was in turn a compilation from
Dares Phrygius, Ovid and Statius. Then Petrarch,
Boccaccio and the Provençal poets are his benefac-
tors: the Romaunt of the Rose is only judicious
translation from William of Lorris and John of
Meung : Troilus and Creseide, from Lollius of Ur-
bino : The Cock and the Fox, from the *Lais* of
Marie : The House of Fame, from the French or
Italian : and poor Gower he uses as if he were only
a brick-kiln or stone-quarry out of which to build
his house. He steals by this apology, — that what
he takes has no worth where he finds it and the
greatest where he leaves it. It has come to be
practically a sort of rule in literature, that a man
having once shown himself capable of original writing, is entitled thenceforth to steal from the writings of others at discretion. Thought is the property of him who can entertain it and of him who can
adequately place it. A certain awkwardness marks
the use of borrowed thoughts; but as soon as we
have learned what to do with them they become our
own.

Thus all originality is relative. Every thinker is

retrospective. The learned member of the legisla-
ture, at Westminster or at Washington, speaks and
votes for thousands. Show us the constituency, and
the now invisible channels by which the senator is
made aware of their wishes; the crowd of practical
and knowing men, who, by correspondence or conversation, are feeding him with evidence, anecdotes
and estimates, and it will bereave his fine attitude
and resistance of something of their impressiveness.
As Sir Robert Peel and Mr. Webster vote, so
Locke and Rousseau think, for thousands; and so
there were fountains all around Homer, Menu,
Saadi, or Milton, from which they drew; friends,
lovers, books, traditions, proverbs, — all perished
— which, if seen, would go to reduce the wonder.
Did the bard speak with authority? Did he feel
himself overmatched by any companion? The ap-
peal is to the consciousness of the writer. Is there
at last in his breast a Delphi whereof to ask concerning any thought or thing, whether it be verily
so, yea or nay? and to have answer, and to rely on
that? All the debts which such a man could contract to other wit would never disturb his consciousness of originality; for the ministrations of books
and of other minds are a whiff of smoke to that
most private reality with which he has conversed.
It is easy to see that what is best written or
done by genius in the world, was no man's work,

but came by wide social labor, when a thousand wrought like one, sharing the same impulse. Our English Bible is a wonderful specimen of the strength and music of the English language. But it was not made by one man, or at one time; but centuries and churches brought it to perfection. There never was a time when there was not some translation existing. The Liturgy, admired for its energy and pathos, is an anthology of the piety of ages and nations, a translation of the prayers and forms of the Catholic church, — these collected, too, in long periods, from the prayers and meditations of every saint and sacred writer all over the world. Grotius makes the like remark in respect to the Lord's Prayer, that the single clauses of which it is composed were already in use in the time of Christ, in the Rabbinical forms. He picked out the grains of gold. The nervous language of the Common Law, the impressive forms of our courts and the precision and substantial truth of the legal distinctions, are the contribution of all the sharp-sighted, strong-minded men who have lived in the countries where these laws govern. The translation of Plutarch gets its excellence by being translation on translation. There never was a time when there was none. All the truly idiomatic and national phrases are kept, and all others successively picked out and thrown away.

Something like the same process had gone on, long before, with the originals of these books. The world takes liberties with world - books. Vedas, Æsop's Fables, Pilpay, Arabian Nights, Cid, Iliad, Robin Hood, Scottish Minstrelsy, are not the work of single men. In the composition of such works the time thinks, the market thinks, the mason, the carpenter, the merchant, the farmer, the fop, all think for us. Every book supplies its time with one good word ; every municipal law, every trade, every folly of the day; and the generic catholic genius who is not afraid or ashamed to owe his originality to the originality of all, stands with the next age as the recorder and embodiment of his own.

We have to thank the researches of antiquaries, and the Shakspeare Society, for ascertaining the steps of the English drama, from the Mysteries celebrated in churches and by churchmen, and the final detachment from the church, and the completion of secular plays, from Ferrex and Porrex, and Gammer Gurton's Needle, down to the possession of the stage by the very pieces which Shakspeare altered, remodelled and finally made his own. Elated with success and piqued by the growing interest of the problem, they have left no bookstall unsearched, no chest in a garret unopened, no file of old yellow accounts to decompose in

damp and worms, so keen was the hope to discover whether the boy Shakspeare poached or not,
whether he held horses at the theatre door, whether
he kept school, and why he left in his will only his
second-best bed to Ann Hathaway, his wife.

There is somewhat touching in the madness with
which the passing age mischooses the object on
which all candles shine and all eyes are turned;
the care with which it registers every trifle touching Queen Elizabeth and King James, and the
Essexes, Leicesters, Burleighs and Buckinghams;
and lets pass without a single valuable note the
founder of another dynasty, which alone will cause
the Tudor dynasty to be remembered, — the man
who carries the Saxon race in him by the inspiration which feeds him, and on whose thoughts the
foremost people of the world are now for some ages
to be nourished, and minds to receive this and not
another bias. A popular player; — nobody suspected he was the poet of the human race; and the
secret was kept as faithfully from poets and intellectual men as from courtiers and frivolous people.
Bacon, who took the inventory of the human understanding for his times, never mentioned his
name. Ben Jonson, though we have strained his
few words of regard and panegyric, had no suspi-
cion of the elastic fame whose first vibrations he
was attempting. He no doubt thought the praise

he has conceded to him generous, and esteemed
himself, out of all question, the better poet of the
two.

If it need wit to know wit, according to the proverb, Shakspeare's time should be capable of recog-
nizing it. Sir Henry Wotton was born four years
after Shakspeare, and died twenty-three years after
him; and I find, among his correspondents and
acquaintances, the following persons: Theodore
Beza, Isaac Casaubon, Sir Philip Sidney, the
Earl of Essex, Lord Bacon, Sir Walter Raleigh,
John Milton, Sir Henry Vane, Isaac Walton, Dr.
Donne, Abraham Cowley, Bellarmine, Charles
Cotton, John Pym, John Hales, Kepler, Vieta, Al-
bericus Gentilis, Paul Sarpi, Arminius; with all
of whom exists some token of his having commu-
nicated, without enumerating many others whom
doubtless he saw, — Shakspeare, Spenser, Jonson,
Beaumont, Massinger, the two Herberts, Marlow,
Chapman and the rest. Since the constellation of
great men who appeared in Greece in the time of
Pericles, there was never any such society; — yet
their genius failed them to find out the best head
in the universe. Our poet's mask was impenetra-
ble. You cannot see the mountain near. It took
a century to make it suspected; and not until two
centuries had passed, after his death, did any criticism which we think adequate begin to appear. It

was not possible to write the history of Shakspeare till now; for he is the father of German literature : it was with the introduction of Shakspeare into German, by Lessing, and the translation of his works by Wieland and Schlegel, that the rapid burst of German literature was most intimately connected. It was not until the nineteenth century, whose speculative genius is a sort of living Hamlet, that the tragedy of Hamlet could find such wondering readers. Now, literature, philosophy and thought, are Shakspearized. His mind is the horizon beyond which, at present, we do not see. Our ears are educated to music by his rhythm. Coleridge and Goethe are the only critics who have expressed our convictions with any adequate fidelity : but there is in all cultivated minds a silent appreciation of his superlative power and beauty, which, like Christianity, qualifies the period.

The Shakspeare Society have inquired in all directions, advertised the missing facts, offered money for any information that will lead to proof, — and with what result? Beside some important illustration of the history of the English stage, to which I have adverted, they have gleaned a few facts touching the property, and dealings in regard to property, of the poet. It appears that from year to year he owned a larger share in the Blackfriars'

Theatre: its wardrobe and other appurtenances were his: that he bought an estate in his native village with his earnings as writer and shareholder; that he lived in the best house in Stratford; was intrusted by his neighbors with their commissions in London, as of borrowing money, and the like; that he was a veritable farmer. About the time when he was writing Macbeth, he sues Philip Rogers, in the borough-court of Stratford, for thirty-five shillings, ten pence, for corn delivered to him at different times; and in all respects appears as a good husband, with no reputation for eccentricity or excess. He was a good-natured sort of man, an actor and shareholder in the theatre, not in any striking manner distinguished from other actors and managers. I admit the importance of this information. It was well worth the pains that have been taken to procure it.

But whatever scraps of information concerning his condition these researches may have rescued, they can shed no light upon that infinite invention which is the concealed magnet of his attraction for us. We are very clumsy writers of history. We tell the chronicle of parentage, birth, birth-place, schooling, school-mates, earning of money, marriage, publication of books, celebrity, death; and when we have come to an end of this gossip, no ray of relation appears between it and the goddess-

born ; and it seems as if, had we dipped at random
into the " Modern Plutarch," and read any other
life there, it would have fitted the poems as well.
It is the essence of poetry to spring, like the rain-
bow daughter of Wonder, from the invisible, to
abolish the past and refuse all history.   Malone,
Warburton, Dyce and Collier, have wasted their oil.
The famed theatres, Covent Garden, Drury Lane,
the Park and Tremont have vainly assisted.   Bet-
terton, Garrick, Kemble, Kean and Macready dedicate their lives to this genius; him they crown,
elucidate, obey and express.   The genius knows
them not.   The recitation begins ; one golden word
leaps out immortal from all this painted pedantry
and sweetly torments us with invitations to its own
inaccessible homes.   I remember I went once to
see the Hamlet of a famed performer, the pride of
the English stage ; and all I then heard and all I
now remember of the tragedian was that in which
the tragedian had no part; simply Hamlet's question to the ghost : —

> " What may this mean,
> That thou, dead corse, again in complete steel
> Revisit'st thus the glimpses of the moon ? "

That imagination which dilates the closet he writes
in to the world's dimension, crowds it with agents
in rank and order, as quickly reduces the big reality to be the glimpses of the moon.   These tricks

of his magic spoil for us the illusions of the green-room. Can any biography shed light on the localities into which the Midsummer Night's Dream admits me? Did Shakspeare confide to any notary or parish recorder, sacristan, or surrogate in Stratford, the genesis of that delicate creation? The forest of Arden, the nimble air of Scone Castle, the moonlight of Portia's villa, " the antres vast and desarts idle " of Othello's captivity, — where is the third cousin, or grand-nephew, the chancellor's file of accounts, or private letter, that has kept one word of those transcendent secrets? In fine, in this drama, as in all great works of art, — in the Cyclopæan architecture of Egypt and India, in the Phidian sculpture, the Gothic minsters, the Italian painting, the Ballads of Spain and Scotland, — the Genius draws up the ladder after him, when the creative age goes up to heaven, and gives way to a new age, which sees the works and asks in vain for a history.

Shakspeare is the only biographer of Shakspeare; and even he can tell nothing, except to the Shakspeare in us, that is, to our most apprehensive and sympathetic hour. He cannot step from off his tripod and give us anecdotes of his inspirations. Read the antique documents extricated, analyzed and compared by the assiduous Dyce and Collier, and now read one of these skyey

sentences, — aerolites, — which seem to have fallen
out of heaven, and which not your experience but
the man within the breast has accepted as words
of fate, and tell me if they match; if the former
account in any manner for the latter; or which
gives the most historical insight into the man.

Hence, though our external history is so meagre,
yet, with Shakspeare for biographer, instead of
Aubrey and Rowe, we have really the information
which is material; that which describes character
and fortune, that which, if we were about to meet
the man and deal with him, would most import
us to know. We have his recorded convictions
on those questions which knock for answer at every
heart, — on life and death, on love, on wealth and
poverty, on the prizes of life and the ways whereby
we come at them; on the characters of men, and
the influences, occult and open, which affect their
fortunes; and on those mysterious and demoniacal
powers which defy our science and which yet in-
terweave their malice and their gift in our bright-
est hours. Who ever read the volume of the
Sonnets without finding that the poet had there
revealed, under masks that are no masks to the
intelligent, the lore of friendship and of love; the
confusion of sentiments in the most susceptible,
and, at the same time, the most intellectual of
men? What trait of his private mind has he

hidden in his dramas? One can discern, in his ample pictures of the gentleman and the king, what forms and humanities pleased him; his delight in troops of friends, in large hospitality, in cheerful giving. Let Timon, let Warwick, let Antonio the merchant answer for his great heart. So far from Shakspeare's being the least known, he is the one person, in all modern history, known to us. What point of morals, of manners, of economy, of philosophy, of religion, of taste, of the conduct of life, has he not settled? What mystery has he not signified his knowledge of? What office, or function, or district of man's work, has he not remembered? What king has he not taught state, as Talma taught Napoleon? What maiden has not found him finer than her delicacy? What lover has he not outloved? What sage has he not outseen? What gentleman has he not instructed in the rudeness of his behavior?

Some able and appreciating critics think no criticism on Shakspeare valuable that does not rest purely on the dramatic merit; that he is falsely judged as poet and philosopher. I think as highly as these critics of his dramatic merit, but still think it secondary. He was a full man, who liked to talk; a brain exhaling thoughts and images, which, seeking vent, found the drama next

at hand. Had he been less, we should have had
to consider how well he filled his place, how good
a dramatist he was, — and he is the best in the
world. But it turns out that what he has to
say is of that weight as to withdraw some attention
from the vehicle; and he is like some saint whose
history is to be rendered into all languages, into
verse and prose, into songs and pictures, and cut
up into proverbs; so that the occasion which gave
the saint's meaning the form of a conversation, or
of a prayer, or of a code of laws, is immaterial
compared with the universality of its application.
So it fares with the wise Shakspeare and his book
of life. He wrote the airs for all our modern
music: he wrote the text of modern life; the text
of manners: he drew the man of England and
Europe; the father of the man in America; he
drew the man, and described the day, and what is
done in it: he read the hearts of men and women,
their probity, and their second thought and wiles;
the wiles of innocence, and the transitions by
which virtues and vices slide into their contraries:
he could divide the mother's part from the father's
part in the face of the child, or draw the fine
demarcations of freedom and of fate: he knew
the laws of repression which make the police of
nature: and all the sweets and all the terrors of
human lot lay in his mind as truly but as softly

as the landscape lies on the eye. And the importance of this wisdom of life sinks the form, as of
Drama or Epic, out of notice. 'T is like making
a question concerning the paper on which a king's
message is written.

Shakspeare is as much out of the category of
eminent authors, as he is out of the crowd. He
is inconceivably wise; the others, conceivably. A
good reader can, in a sort, nestle into Plato's brain
and think from thence; but not into Shakspeare's.
We are still out of doors. For executive faculty,
for creation, Shakspeare is unique. No man can
imagine it better. He was the farthest reach of
subtlety compatible with an individual self, — the
subtilest of authors, and only just within the possibility of authorship. With this wisdom of life
is the equal endowment of imaginative and of
lyric power. He clothed the creatures of his
legend with form and sentiments as if they were
people who had lived under his roof; and few
real men have left such distinct characters as these
fictions. And they spoke in language as sweet
as it was fit. Yet his talents never seduced him
into an ostentation, nor did he harp on one string.
An omnipresent humanity co-ordinates all his faculties. Give a man of talents a story to tell, and
his partiality will presently appear. He has certain observations, opinions, topics, which have

some accidental prominence, and which he disposes all to exhibit. He crams this part and
starves that other part, consulting not the fitness
of the thing, but his fitness and strength. But
Shakspeare has no peculiarity, no importunate
topic; but all is duly given; no veins, no curiosi-
ties; no cow-painter, no bird-fancier, no manner-
ist is he: he has no discoverable egotism: the
great he tells greatly; the small subordinately.
He is wise without emphasis or assertion; he is
strong, as nature is strong, who lifts the land into
mountain slopes without effort and by the same
rule as she floats a bubble in the air, and likes as
well to do the one as the other. This makes that
equality of power in farce, tragedy, narrative and
love-songs; a merit so incessant that each reader
is incredulous of the perception of other readers.

This power of expression, or of transferring the
inmost truth of things into music and verse, makes
him the type of the poet and has added a new
problem to metaphysics. This is that which throws
him into natural history, as a main production of
the globe, and as announcing new eras and amelio-
rations. Things were mirrored in his poetry without loss or blur: he could paint the fine with precision, the great with compass, the tragic and the
comic indifferently and without any distortion or
favor. He carried his powerful execution into

minute details, to a hair point; finishes an eyelash or a dimple as firmly as he draws a mountain; and yet these, like nature's, will bear the scrutiny of the solar microscope.

In short, he is the chief example to prove that more or less of production, more or fewer pictures, is a thing indifferent. He had the power to make one picture. Daguerre learned how to let one flower etch its image on his plate of iodine, and then proceeds at leisure to etch a million. There are always objects; but there was never representation. Here is perfect representation, at last; and now let the world of figures sit for their portraits. No recipe can be given for the making of a Shakspeare; but the possibility of the translation of things into song is demonstrated.

His lyric power lies in the genius of the piece. The sonnets, though their excellence is lost in the splendor of the dramas, are as inimitable as they; and it is not a merit of lines, but a total merit of the piece; like the tone of voice of some incomparable person, so is this a speech of poetic beings, and any clause as unproducible now as a whole poem.

Though the speeches in the plays, and single lines, have a beauty which tempts the ear to pause on them for their euphuism, yet the sentence is so loaded with meaning and so linked with its

foregoers and followers, that the logician is satisfied. His means are as admirable as his ends;
every subordinate invention, by which he helps
himself to connect some irreconcilable opposites,
is a poem too. He is not reduced to dismount and
walk because his horses are running off with him
in some distant direction : he always rides.

The finest poetry was first experience; but the
thought has suffered a transformation since it was
an experience. Cultivated men often attain a good
degree of skill in writing verses; but it is easy to
read, through their poems, their personal history:
any one acquainted with the parties can name every
figure; this is Andrew and that is Rachel. The
sense thus remains prosaic. It is a caterpillar
with wings, and not yet a butterfly. In the poet's
mind the fact has gone quite over into the new
element of thought, and has lost all that is exuvial.
This generosity abides with Shakspeare. We say,
from the truth and closeness of his pictures, that he
knows the lesson by heart. Yet there is not a
trace of egotism.

One more royal trait properly belongs to the
poet. I mean his cheerfulness, without which no
man can be a poet, — for beauty is his aim. He
loves virtue, not for its obligation but for its grace:
he delights in the world, in man, in woman, for the
lovely light that sparkles from them. Beauty, the

spirit of joy and hilarity, he sheds over the universe. Epicurus relates that poetry hath such charms that a lover might forsake his mistress to partake of them. And the true bards have been noted for their firm and cheerful temper. Homer lies in sunshine; Chaucer is glad and erect; and Saadi says, "It was rumored abroad that I was penitent; but what had I to do with repentance?" Not less sovereign and cheerful, — much more sovereign and cheerful, is the tone of Shakspeare. His name suggests joy and emancipation to the heart of men. If he should appear in any company of human souls, who would not march in his troop? He touches nothing that does not borrow health and longevity from his festal style.

And now, how stands the account of man with this bard and benefactor, when, in solitude, shutting our ears to the reverberations of his fame, we seek to strike the balance? Solitude has austere lessons; it can teach us to spare both heroes and poets; and it weighs Shakspeare also, and finds him to share the halfness and imperfection of humanity.

Shakspeare, Homer, Dante, Chaucer, saw the splendor of meaning that plays over the visible world; knew that a tree had another use than for apples, and corn another than for meal, and the ball of the earth, than for tillage and roads: that these things bore a second and finer harvest to the mind, being emblems of its thoughts, and conveying in all their natural history a certain mute commentary on human life. Shakspeare employed them as colors to compose his picture. He rested in their beauty; and never took the step which seemed inevitable to such genius, namely to explore the virtue which resides in these symbols and imparts this power : — what is that which they themselves say ? He converted the elements which waited on his command, into entertainments. He was master of the revels to mankind. Is it not as if one should have, through majestic powers of science, the comets given into his hand, or the planets and their moons, and should draw them from their orbits to glare with the municipal fireworks on a holiday night, and advertise in all towns, " Very superior pyrotechny this evening " ? Are the agents of nature, and the power to understand them, worth no more than a street serenade, or the breath of a cigar ? One remembers again the trumpet-text in the Koran, — " The heavens and the earth and all that is between them, think ye we have created them in jest?" As long as the question is of talent and mental power, the world of men has not his equal to show. But when the question is, to life and its materials and its auxiliaries, how does he profit me ? What does it signify? It is but a Twelfth Night, or Midsummer-Night's Dream, or Winter Evening's Tale: what signifies another picture more or less? The Egyptian verdict of the Shakspeare Societies comes to mind; that he was a jovial actor and manager. I can not marry this fact to his verse. Other admirable men have led lives in some sort of keeping with their thought; but this man, in wide contrast. Had he been less, had he reached only the common measure of great authors, of Bacon, Milton, Tasso, Cervantes, we might leave the fact in the twilight of human fate: but that this man of men, he who gave to the science of mind a new and larger subject than had ever existed, and planted the standard of humanity some furlongs forward into Chaos, — that he should not be wise for himself; — it must even go into the world's history that the best poet led an obscure and profane life, using his genius for the public amusement.

Well, other men, priest and prophet, Israelite, German and Swede, beheld the same objects: they also saw through them that which was contained. And to what purpose? The beauty straightway vanished; they read commandments, all-excluding mountainous duty; an obligation, a sadness, as of piled mountains, fell on them, and life became ghastly, joyless, a pilgrim's progress, a probation, beleaguered round with doleful histories of Adam's fall and curse behind us; with doomsdays and purgatorial and penal fires before us; and the heart of the seer and the heart of the listener sank in them.

It must be conceded that these are half-views of half-men. The world still wants its poet-priest, a reconciler, who shall not trifle, with Shakspeare the player, nor shall grope in graves, with Swedenborg the mourner; but who shall see, speak, and act, with equal inspiration. [For knowledge will brighten the sunshine; right is more beautiful than private affection; and love is compatible with universal wisdom.]

NAPOLEON; OR, THE MAN OF THE WORLD.

VI.

NAPOLEON; OR, THE MAN OF THE WORLD.

———•———

AMONG the eminent persons of the nineteenth century, Bonaparte is far the best known and the most powerful; and owes his predominance to the fidelity with which he expresses the tone of thought and belief, the aims of the masses of active and cultivated men. It is Swedenborg's theory that every organ is made up of homogeneous particles; or as it is sometimes expressed, every whole is made of similars; that is, the lungs are composed of infinitely small lungs; the liver, of infinitely small livers; the kidney, of little kidneys, &c. Following this analogy, if any man is found to carry with him the power and affections of vast numbers, if Napoleon is France, if Napoleon is Europe, it is because the people whom he sways are little Napoleons.

In our society there is a standing antagonism between the conservative and the democratic classes; between those who have made their

fortunes, and the young and the poor who have
fortunes to make; between the interests of dead
labor, — that is, the labor of hands long ago still
in the grave, which labor is now entombed in
money stocks, or in land and buildings owned by
idle capitalists, — and the interests of living labor,
which seeks to possess itself of land and buildings
and money stocks. The first class is timid, selfish, illiberal, hating innovation, and continually
losing numbers by death. The second class is
selfish also, encroaching, bold, self-relying, always
outnumbering the other and recruiting its numbers every hour by births. It desires to keep
open every avenue to the competition of all, and
to multiply avenues: the class of business men in
America, in England, in France and throughout
Europe; the class of industry and skill. Napoleon is its representative. The instinct of active, brave, able men, throughout the middle class
every where, has pointed out Napoleon as the incarnate Democrat. He had their virtues and their
vices; above all, he had their spirit or aim. That
tendency is material, pointing at a sensual success and employing the richest and most various
means to that end; conversant with mechanical
powers, highly intellectual, widely and accurately
learned and skilful, but subordinating all intellectual and spiritual forces into means to a mate-

rial success. To be the rich man, is the end.
"God has granted," says the Koran, "to every
people a prophet in its own tongue." Paris and
London and New York, the spirit of commerce, of
money and material power, were also to have their
prophet; and Bonaparte was qualified and sent.

Every one of the million readers of anecdotes
or memoirs or lives of Napoleon, delights in the
page, because he studies in it his own history.
Napoleon is thoroughly modern, and, at the highest point of his fortunes, has the very spirit of
the newspapers. He is no saint, — to use his
own word, "no capuchin," and he is no hero, in
the high sense. The man in the street finds in
him the qualities and powers of other men in the
street. He finds him, like himself, by birth a
citizen, who, by very intelligible merits, arrived
at such a commanding position that he could indulge all those tastes which the common man
possesses but is obliged to conceal and deny:
good society, good books, fast travelling, dress,
dinners, servants without number, personal weight,
the execution of his ideas, the standing in the
attitude of a benefactor to all persons about him,
the refined enjoyments of pictures, statues, music,
palaces and conventional honors, — precisely what
is agreeable to the heart of every man in the nineteenth century, this powerful man possessed.

It is true that a man of Napoleon's truth of adaptation to the mind of the masses around him, becomes not merely representative but actually a monopolizer and usurper of other minds. Thus Mirabeau plagiarized every good thought, every good word that was spoken in France. Dumont relates that he sat in the gallery of the Convention and heard Mirabeau make a speech. It struck Dumont that he could fit it with a peroration, which he wrote in pencil immediately, and showed it to Lord Elgin, who sat by him. Lord Elgin approved it, and Dumont, in the evening, showed it to Mirabeau. Mirabeau read it, pronounced it admirable, and declared he would incorporate it into his harangue to-morrow, to the Assembly. "It is impossible," said Dumont, "as, unfortunately, I have shown it to Lord Elgin." "If you have shown it to Lord Elgin and to fifty persons beside, I shall still speak it to-morrow:" and he did speak it, with much effect, at the next day's session. For Mirabeau, with his overpowering personality, felt that these things which his presence inspired were as much his own as if he had said them, and that his adoption of them gave them their weight. Much more absolute and centralizing was the successor to Mirabeau's popularity and to much more than his predominance in France. Indeed, a man of Napoleon's stamp

almost ceases to have a private speech and opinion. He is so largely receptive, and is so placed,
that he comes to be a bureau for all the intelligence, wit and power of the age and country. He
gains the battle; he makes the code; he makes
the system of weights and measures; he levels the
Alps; he builds the road. All distinguished en-
gineers, savans, statists, report to him: so likewise
do all good heads in every kind: he adopts the
best measures, sets his stamp on them, and not
these alone, but on every happy and memorable
expression. Every sentence spoken by Napoleon
and every line of his writing, deserves reading,
as it is the sense of France.

Bonaparte was the idol of common men because
he had in transcendent degree the qualities and
powers of common men. There is a certain satisfaction in coming down to the lowest ground of
politics, for we get rid of cant and hypocrisy.
Bonaparte wrought, in common with that great
class he represented, for power and wealth, — but
Bonaparte, specially, without any scruple as to the
means. All the sentiments which embarrass men's
pursuit of these objects, he set aside. The sentiments were for women and children. Fontanes, in
1804, expressed Napoleon's own sense, when in behalf of the Senate he addressed him, — "Sire, the
desire of perfection is the worst disease that ever

afflicted the human mind." The advocates of liberty and of progress are " ideologists ; " — a word of contempt often in his mouth ; — " Necker is an ideologist : " " Lafayette is an ideologist."

An Italian proverb, too well known, declares that " if you would succeed, you must not be too good." It is an advantage, within certain limits, to have renounced the dominion of the sentiments of piety, gratitude and generosity : since what was an impassable bar to us, and still is to others, becomes a convenient weapon for our purposes ; just as the river which was a formidable barrier, winter transforms into the smoothest of roads.

Napoleon renounced, once for all, sentiments and affections, and would help himself with his hands and his head. With him is no miracle and no magic. He is a worker in brass, in iron, in wood, in earth, in roads, in buildings, in money and in troops, and a very consistent and wise master-workman. He is never weak and literary, but acts with the solidity and the precision of natural agents. He has not lost his native sense and sympathy with things. Men give way before such a man, as before natural events. To be sure there are men enough who are immersed in things, as farmers, smiths, sailors and mechanics generally ; and we know how real and solid such men appear in the presence of scholars and grammarians : but these

men ordinarily lack the power of arrangement, and
are like hands without a head. But Bonaparte su-
peradded to this mineral and animal force, insight
and generalization, so that men saw in him combined the natural and the intellectual power, as if
the sea and land had taken flesh and begun to cipher. Therefore the land and sea seem to presup-
pose him. He came unto his own and they received him. This ciphering operative knows what
he is working with and what is the product. He
knew the properties of gold and iron, of wheels and
ships, of troops and diplomatists, and required that
each should do after its kind.

The art of war was the game in which he exerted
his arithmetic. It consisted, according to him, in
having always more forces than the enemy, on the
point where the enemy is attacked, or where he attacks: and his whole talent is strained by endless
manœuvre and evolution, to march always on the
enemy at an angle, and destroy his forces in detail.
It is obvious that a very small force, skilfully and
rapidly manœuvring so as always to bring two men
against one at the point of engagement, will be an
overmatch for a much larger body of men.

The times, his constitution and his early circumstances combined to develop this pattern democrat.
He had the virtues of his class and the conditions
for their activity. That common-sense which **no**

sooner respects any end than it finds the means to
effect it; the delight in the use of means; in the
choice, simplification and combining of means; the
directness and thoroughness of his work; the prudence with which all was seen and the energy with
which all was done, make him the natural organ
and head of what I may almost call, from its extent, the *modern* party.

Nature must have far the greatest share in every
success, and so in his. Such a man was wanted,
and such a man was born; a man of stone and
iron, capable of sitting on horseback sixteen or seventeen hours, of going many days together without
rest or food except by snatches, and with the speed
and spring of a tiger in action; a man not embarrassed by any scruples; compact, instant, selfish,
prudent, and of a perception which did not suffer
itself to be baulked or misled by any pretences of
others, or any superstition or any heat or haste of
his own. "My hand of iron" he said, "was not at
the extremity of my arm, it was immediately connected with my head." He respected the power
of nature and fortune, and ascribed to it his superiority, instead of valuing himself, like inferior
men, on his opinionativeness, and waging war with
nature. His favorite rhetoric lay in allusion to his
star; and he pleased himself, as well as the people,
when he styled himself the "Child of Destiny."

" They charge me," he said, " with the commission of great crimes : men of my stamp do not commit crimes. Nothing has been more simple than my elevation, 't is in vain to ascribe it to intrigue or crime ; it was owing to the peculiarity of the times and to my reputation of having fought well against the enemies of my country. I have always marched with the opinion of great masses and with events. Of what use then would crimes be to me ? " Again he said, speaking of his son, " My son can not replace me ; I could not replace myself. I am the creature of circumstances."

He had a directness of action never before combined with so much comprehension. He is a realist, terrific to all talkers and confused truth-obscuring persons. He sees where the matter hinges, throws himself on the precise point of resistance, and slights all other considerations. He is strong in the right manner, namely by insight. He never blundered into victory, but won his battles in his head before he won them on the field. His principal means are in himself. He asks counsel of no other. In 1796 he writes to the Directory : " I have conducted the campaign without consulting any one. I should have done no good if I had been under the necessity of conforming to the notions of another person. I have gained some advantages over superior forces and when totally destitute of every thing, because, in the persuasion that your confidence was reposed in me, my actions were as prompt as my thoughts."

History is full, down to this day, of the imbecility of kings and governors. They are a class of persons much to be pitied, for they know not what they should do. The weavers strike for bread, and the king and his ministers, knowing not what to do, meet them with bayonets. But Napoleon understood his business. Here was a man who in each moment and emergency knew what to do next. It is an immense comfort and refreshment to the spirits, not only of kings, but of citizens. Few men have any next; they live from hand to mouth, without plan, and are ever at the end of their line, and after each action wait for an impulse from abroad. Napoleon had been the first man of the world, if his ends had been purely public. As he is, he inspires confidence and vigor by the extraordinary unity of his action. He is firm, sure, self-denying, self-postponing, sacrificing every thing, — money, troops, generals, and his own safety also, to his aim; not misled, like common adventurers, by the splendor of his own means. "Incidents ought not to govern policy," he said, "but policy, incidents." "To be hurried away by every event is to have no political system at all." His victories were only so many doors, and he never for a

moment lost sight of his way onward, in the dazzle and uproar of the present circumstance. He
knew what to do, and he flew to his mark. He
would shorten a straight line to come at his object.
Horrible anecdotes may no doubt be collected from
his history, of the price at which he bought his successes ; but he must not therefore be set down as
cruel, but only as one who knew no impediment to
his will; not bloodthirsty, not cruel, — but woe to
what thing or person stood in his way ! Not bloodthirsty, but not sparing of blood, — and pitiless.
He saw only the object: the obstacle must give
way. " Sire, General Clarke can not combine with
General Junot, for the dreadful fire of the Austrian battery." — " Let him carry the battery."
— " Sire, every regiment that approaches the heavy
artillery is sacrificed: Sire, what orders ? "— " Forward, forward ! " Seruzier, a colonel of artillery,
gives, in his " Military Memoirs," the following
sketch of a scene after the battle of Austerlitz. —
" At the moment in which the Russian army was
making its retreat, painfully, but in good order, on
the ice of the lake, the Emperor Napoleon came
riding at full speed toward the artillery. " You
are losing time," he cried; "fire upon those masses;
they must be engulfed: fire upon the ice ! " The
order remained unexecuted for ten minutes. In
vain several officers and myself were placed on the

slope of a hill to produce the effect : their balls and mine rolled upon the ice without breaking it up. Seeing that, I tried a simple method of elevating light howitzers. The almost perpendicular fall of the heavy projectiles produced the desired effect. My method was immediately followed by the adjoining batteries, and in less than no time we buried " some [1] " thousands of Russians and Austrians under the waters of the lake."

In the plenitude of his resources, every obstacle seemed to vanish. "There shall be no Alps," he said ; and he built his perfect roads, climbing by graded galleries their steepest precipices, until Italy was as open to Paris as any town in France. He laid his bones to, and wrought for his crown. Having decided what was to be done, he did that with might and main. He put out all his strength. He risked every thing and spared nothing, neither ammunition, nor money, nor troops, nor generals, nor himself.

We like to see every thing do its office after its kind, whether it be a milch-cow or a rattle-snake ; and if fighting be the best mode of adjusting national differences, (as large majorities of men seem to agree,) certainly Bonaparte was right in making it thorough. The grand principle of war,

---

[1] As I quote at second hand, and cannot procure Seruzier, I dare not adopt the high figure I find.

he said, was that an army ought always to be ready, by day and by night and at all hours, to make all the resistance it is capable of making. He never economized his ammunition, but, on a hostile position, rained a torrent of iron, — shells, balls, grape-shot, — to annihilate all defence. On any point of resistance he concentrated squadron on squadron in overwhelming numbers until it was swept out of existence. To a regiment of horse-chasseurs at Lobenstein, two days before the battle of Jena, Napoleon said, " My lads, you must not fear death ; when soldiers brave death, they drive him into the enemy's ranks." In the fury of assault, he no more spared himself. He went to the edge of his possibility. It is plain that in Italy he did what he could, and all that he could. He came, several times, within an inch of ruin ; and his own person was all but lost. He was flung into the marsh at Arcola. The Austrians were between him and his troops, in the *mêlée*, and he was brought off with desperate efforts. At Lonato, and at other places, he was on the point of being taken prisoner. He fought sixty battles. He had never enough. Each victory was a new weapon. " My power would fall, were I not to support it by new achievements. Conquest has made me what I am, and conquest must maintain me." He felt, with every wise man, that as much life is needed for conserva⸗

tion as for creation. We are always in peril, always in a bad plight, just on the edge of destruction and only to be saved by invention and courage.

This vigor was guarded and tempered by the coldest prudence and punctuality. A thunderbolt in the attack, he was found invulnerable in his intrenchments. His very attack was never the inspiration of courage, but the result of calculation. His idea of the best defence consists in being still the attacking party. " My ambition," he says, " was great, but was of a cold nature." In one of his conversations with Las Casas, he remarked, " As to moral courage, I have rarely met with the two-o'clock-in-the-morning kind : I mean unprepared courage ; that which is necessary on an unexpected occasion, and which, in spite of the most unforeseen events, leaves full freedom of judgment and decision : " and he did not hesitate to declare that he was himself eminently endowed with this two-o'clock-in-the-morning courage, and that he had met with few persons equal to himself in this respect.

Every thing depended on the nicety of his combinations, and the stars were not more punctual than his arithmetic. His personal attention descended to the smallest particulars. " At Montebello, I ordered Kellermann to attack with eight hundred horse, and with these he separated the six thousand Hungarian grenadiers, before the very eyes of the Austrian cavalry. This cavalry was half a league off and required a quarter of an hour to arrive on the field of action, and I have observed that it is always these quarters of an hour that decide the fate of a battle." "Before he fought a battle, Bonaparte thought little about what he should do in case of success, but a great deal about what he should do in case of a reverse of fortune." The same prudence and good sense mark all his behavior. His instructions to his secretary at the Tuileries are worth remembering. "During the night, enter my chamber as seldom as possible. Do not awake me when you have any good news to communicate; with that there is no hurry. But when you bring bad news, rouse me instantly, for then there is not a moment to be lost." It was a whimsical economy of the same kind which dictated his practice, when general in Italy, in regard to his burdensome correspondence. He directed Bourrienne to leave all letters unopened for three weeks, and then observed with satisfaction how large a part of the correspondence had thus disposed of itself and no longer required an answer. His achievement of business was immense, and enlarges the known powers of man. There have been many working kings, from Ulysses to William of Orange, but none who accomplished a tithe of this man's performance.

To these gifts of nature, Napoleon added the advantage of having been born to a private and humble fortune. In his later days he had the weakness of wishing to add to his crowns and badges the prescription of aristocracy; but he knew his debt to his austere education, and made no secret of his contempt for the born kings, and for " the hereditary asses," as he coarsely styled the Bourbons. He said that " in their exile they had learned nothing, and forgot nothing." Bonaparte had passed through all the degrees of military service, but also was citizen before he was emperor, and so has the key to citizenship. His remarks and estimates discover the information and justness of measurement of the middle class. Those who had to deal with him found that he was not to be imposed upon, but could cipher as well as another man. This appears in all parts of his Memoirs, dictated at St. Helena. When the expenses of the empress, of his household, of his palaces, had accumulated great debts, Napoleon examined the bills of the creditors himself, detected overcharges and errors, and reduced the claims by considerable sums.

His grand weapon, namely the millions whom he directed, he owed to the representative character which clothed him. He interests us as he stands for France and for Europe; and he exists as captain and king only as far as the Revolution, or the interest of the industrious masses, found an organ and a leader in him. In the social interests, he knew the meaning and value of labor, and threw himself naturally on that side. I like an incident mentioned by one of his biographers at St. Helena. " When walking with Mrs. Balcombe, some servants, carrying heavy boxes, passed by on the road, and Mrs. Balcombe desired them, in rather an angry tone, to keep back. Napoleon interfered, saying ' Respect the burden, Madam.' " In the time of the empire he directed attention to the improvement and embellishment of the markets of the capital. " The market-place," he said, " is the Louvre of the common people." The principal works that have survived him are his magnificent roads. He filled the troops with his spirit, and a sort of freedom and companionship grew up between him and them, which the forms of his court never permitted between the officers and himself. They performed, under his eye, that which no others could do. The best document of his relation to his troops is the order of the day on the morning of the battle of Austerlitz, in which Napoleon promises the troops that he will keep his person out of reach of fire. This declaration, which is the reverse of that ordinarily made by generals and sovereigns on the eve of a battle, sufficiently explains the devotion of the army to their leader.

But though there is in particulars this identity between Napoleon and the mass of the people, his real strength lay in their conviction that he was their representative in his genius and aims, not only when he courted, but when he controlled, and even when he decimated them by his conscriptions. He knew, as well as any Jacobin in France, how to philosophize on liberty and equality; and when allusion was made to the precious blood of centuries, which was spilled by the killing of the Duc d'Enghien, he suggested, " Neither is my blood ditch-water." The people felt that no longer the throne was occupied and the land sucked of its nourishment, by a small class of legitimates, secluded from all community with the children of the soil, and holding the ideas and superstitions of a long-forgotten state of society. Instead of that vampyre, a man of themselves held, in the Tuileries, knowledge and ideas like their own, opening of course to them and their children all places of power and trust. The day of sleepy, selfish policy, ever narrowing the means and opportunities of young men, was ended, and a day of expansion and demand was come. A market for all the powers and productions of man was opened; brilliant prizes glittered in the eyes of youth and talent. The old, iron-bound, feudal France was changed into a young Ohio or New York; and those who smarted under the immediate rigors of the new monarch, pardoned them as the necessary severities of the military system which had driven out the oppressor. And even when the majority of the people had begun to ask whether they had really gained any thing under the exhausting levies of men and money of the new master, the whole talent of the country, in every rank and kindred, took his part and defended him as its natural patron. In 1814, when advised to rely on the higher classes, Napoleon said to those around him, " Gentlemen, in the situation in which I stand, my only nobility is the rabble of the Faubourgs."

Napoleon met this natural expectation. The necessity of his position required a hospitality to every sort of talent, and its appointment to trusts ; and his feeling went along with this policy. Like every superior person, he undoubtedly felt a desire for men and compeers, and a wish to measure his power with other masters, and an impatience of fools and underlings. In Italy, he sought for men and found none. " Good God ! " he said, "how rare men are ! There are eighteen millions in Italy, and I have with difficulty found two, — Dandolo and Melzi." In later years, with larger experience, his respect for mankind was not increased. In a moment of bitterness he said to one of his oldest friends, " Men deserve the contempt with which they inspire me. I have only to

put some gold-lace on the coat of my virtuous re-
publicans and they immediately become just what
I wish them." This impatience at levity was, however, an oblique tribute of respect to those able
persons who commanded his regard not only when
he found them friends and coadjutors but also
when they resisted his will. He could not con-
found Fox and Pitt, Carnot, Lafayette and Bernadotte, with the danglers of his court; and in spite
of the detraction which his systematic egotism dictated toward the great captains who conquered
with and for him, ample acknowledgments are
made by him to Lannes, Duroc, Kleber, Dessaix,
Massena, Murat, Ney and Augereau. If he felt
himself their patron and the founder of their fortunes, as when he said " I made my generals out of
mud," — he could not hide his satisfaction in receiving from them a seconding and support com-
mensurate with the grandeur of his enterprise. In
the Russian campaign he was so much impressed by
the courage and resources of Marshal Ney, that he
said, " I have two hundred millions in my coffers,
and I would give them all for Ney." The characters which he has drawn of several of his marshals
are discriminating, and though they did not content the insatiable vanity of French officers, are no
doubt substantially just. And in fact every species
of merit was sought and advanced under his gov-

ernment. " I know" he said, "the depth and draught of water of every one of my generals." Natural power was sure to be well received at his court. Seventeen men in his time were raised from common soldiers to the rank of king, marshal, duke, or general; and the crosses of his Legion of Honor were given to personal valor, and not to family connexion. " When soldiers have been baptized in the fire of a battle-field, they have all one rank in my eyes."

When a natural king becomes a titular king, every body is pleased and satisfied. The Revolution entitled the strong populace of the Faubourg St. Antoine, and every horse - boy and powder-monkey in the army, to look on Napoleon as flesh of his flesh and the creature of *his* party : but there is something in the success of grand talent which enlists an universal sympathy. For in the prevalence of sense and spirit over stupidity and malversation, all reasonable men have an interest; and as intellectual beings we feel the air purified by the electric shock, when material force is overthrown by intellectual energies. As soon as we are removed out of the reach of local and accidental partialities, Man feels that Napoleon fights for him ; these are honest victories; this strong steam-engine does our work. Whatever appeals to the imagination, by transcending the ordinary limits of

human ability, wonderfully encourages and liber‧
ates us. This capacious head, revolving and dis‧
posing sovereignly trains of affairs, and animating
such multitudes of agents; this eye, which looked
through Europe; this prompt invention; this inex‧
haustible resource: — what events! what romantic
pictures! what strange situations! — when spying
the Alps, by a sunset in the Sicilian sea; drawing
up his army for battle in sight of the Pyramids,
and saying to his troops, "From the tops of those
pyramids, forty centuries look down on you;" ford‧
ing the Red Sea; wading in the gulf of the Isth‧
mus of Suez. On the shore of Ptolemais, gigantic
projects agitated him. "Had Acre fallen, I should
have changed the face of the world." His army,
on the night of the battle of Austerlitz, which was
the anniversary of his inauguration as Emperor,
presented him with a bouquet of forty standards
taken in the fight. Perhaps it is a little puerile,
the pleasure he took in making these contrasts
glaring; as when he pleased himself with making
kings wait in his antechambers, at Tilsit, at Paris
and at Erfurt.

We cannot, in the universal imbecility, indecis‧
ion and indolence of men, sufficiently congratulate
ourselves on this strong and ready actor, who took
occasion by the beard, and showed us how much
may be accomplished by the mere force of such vir‧

tues as all men possess in less degrees; namely, by punctuality, by personal attention, by courage and thoroughness. " The Austrians " he said, " do not know the value of time." I should cite him, in his earlier years, as a model of prudence. His power does not consist in any wild or extravagant force; in any enthusiasm like Mahomet's, or singular power of persuasion; but in the exercise of common-sense on each emergency, instead of abiding by rules and customs. The lesson he teaches is that which vigor always teaches; — that there is always room for it. To what heaps of cowardly doubts is not that man's life an answer. When he appeared it was the belief of all military men that there could be nothing new in war; as it is the belief of men to-day that nothing new can be undertaken in politics, or in church, or in letters, or in trade, or in farming, or in our social manners and customs; and as it is at all times the belief of society that the world is used up. But Bonaparte knew better than society; and moreover knew that he knew better. I think all men know better than they do; know that the institutions we so volubly commend are go-carts and baubles; but they dare not trust their presentiments. Bonaparte relied on his own sense, and did not care a bean for other people's. The world treated his novelties just as it treats everybody's novelties, — made infinite objection, mustered all the impediments; but he snapped his finger at their objections. "What creates great difficulty" he remarks, "in the profession of the land-commander, is the necessity of feeding so many men and animals. If he allows himself to be guided by the commissaries he will never stir, and all his expeditions will fail." An example of his common-sense is what he says of the passage of the Alps in winter, which all writers, one repeating after the other, had described as impracticable. "The winter," says Napoleon, "is not the most unfavorable season for the passage of lofty mountains. The snow is then firm, the weather settled, and there is nothing to fear from avalanches, the real and only danger to be apprehended in the Alps. On those high mountains there are often very fine days in December, of a dry cold, with extreme calmness in the air." Read his account, too, of the way in which battles are gained. "In all battles a moment occurs when the bravest troops, after having made the greatest efforts, feel inclined to run. That terror proceeds from a want of confidence in their own courage, and it only requires a slight opportunity, a pretence, to restore confidence to them. The art is, to give rise to the opportunity and to invent the pretence. At Arcola I won the battle with twenty-five horsemen. I seized that moment of lassitude, gave every man a trumpet, and gained the day with this handful. You see that two armies are two bodies which meet and endeavor to frighten each other; a moment of panic occurs, and that moment must be turned to advantage. When a man has been present in many actions, he distinguishes that moment without difficulty: it is as easy as casting up an addition."

This deputy of the nineteenth century added to his gifts a capacity for speculation on general topics. He delighted in running through the range of practical, of literary and of abstract questions. His opinion is always original and to the purpose. On the voyage to Egypt he liked, after dinner, to fix on three or four persons to support a proposition, and as many to oppose it. He gave a subject, and the discussions turned on questions of religion, the different kinds of government and the art of war. One day he asked whether the planets were inhabited? On another, what was the age of the world? Then he proposed to consider the probability of the destruction of the globe, either by water or by fire: at another time, the truth or fallacy of presentiments, and the interpretation of dreams. He was very fond of talking of religion. In 1806 he conversed with Fournier, bishop of Montpellier, on matters of theology. There were two points on which they could not agree, viz. that of hell, and that of salvation out of the pale of the church. The Emperor told Josephine that he disputed like a devil on these two points, on which the bishop was inexorable. To the philosophers he readily yielded all that was proved against religion as the work of men and time, but he would not hear of materialism. One fine night, on deck, amid a clatter of materialism, Bonaparte pointed to the stars, and said, "You may talk as long as you please, gentlemen, but who made all that?" He delighted in the conversation of men of science, particularly of Monge and Berthollet; but the men of letters he slighted; they were "manufacturers of phrases." Of medicine too he was fond of talking, and with those of its practitioners whom he most esteemed, — with Corvisart at Paris, and with Antonomarchi at St. Helena. "Believe me," he said to the last, "we had better leave off all these remedies: life is a fortress which neither you nor I know anything about. Why throw obstacles in the way of its defence? Its own means are superior to all the apparatus of your laboratories. Corvisart candidly agreed with me that all your filthy mixtures are good for nothing. Medicine is a collection of uncertain prescriptions, the results of which, taken collectively, are more fatal than useful to mankind. Water, air and cleanliness are the chief articles in my pharmacopœia."

His memoirs, dictated to Count Montholon and General Gourgaud at St. Helena, have great value, after all the deduction that it seems is to be made from them on account of his known disingenuousness. He has the good-nature of strength and conscious superiority. I admire his simple, clear narrative of his battles; — good as Cæsar's; his good-natured and sufficiently respectful account of Marshal Wurmser and his other antagonists; and his own equality as a writer to his varying subject. The most agreeable portion is the Campaign in Egypt.

He had hours of thought and wisdom. In intervals of leisure, either in the camp or the palace, Napoleon appears as a man of genius directing on abstract questions the native appetite for truth and the impatience of words he was wont to show in war. He could enjoy every play of invention, a romance, a *bon mot*, as well as a stratagem in a campaign. He delighted to fascinate Josephine and her ladies, in a dim-lighted apartment, by the terrors of a fiction to which his voice and dramatic power lent every addition.

I call Napoleon the agent or attorney of the middle class of modern society; of the throng who fill the markets, shops, counting-houses, manufactories, ships, of the modern world, aiming to be rich. He was the agitator, the destroyer of prescription, the internal improver, the liberal, the radical, the inventor of means, the opener of doors and markets, the subverter of monopoly and abuse. Of course the rich and aristocratic did not like him. England, the centre of capital, and Rome and Austria, centres of tradition and genealogy, opposed him. The consternation of the dull and conservative classes, the terror of the foolish old men and old women of the Roman conclave, who in their despair took hold of any thing, and would cling to red-hot iron, — the vain attempts of statists to amuse and deceive him, of the emperor of Austria to bribe him; and the instinct of the young, ardent and active men every where, which pointed him out as the giant of the middle class, make his history bright and commanding. He had the virtues of the masses of his constituents: he had also their vices. I am sorry that the brilliant picture has its reverse. But that is the fatal quality which we discover in our pursuit of wealth, that it is treacherous, and is bought by the breaking or weakening of the sentiments; and it is inevitable that we should find the same fact in the history of this champion, who proposed to himself simply a brilliant career, without any stipulation or scruple concerning the means.

Bonaparte was singularly destitute of generous sentiments. The highest-placed individual in the most cultivated age and population of the world, — he has not the merit of common truth and honesty. He is unjust to his generals; egotistic and monopolizing; meanly stealing the credit of their great actions from Kellermann, from Bernadotte; intriguing to involve his faithful Junot in hopeless bankruptcy, in order to drive him to a distance from Paris, because the familiarity of his manners offends the new pride of his throne. He is a boundless liar. The official paper, his " Moniteur," and all his bulletins, are proverbs for saying what he wished to be believed; and worse, — he sat, in his premature old age, in his lonely island, coldly falsifying facts and dates and characters, and giving to history a theatrical *éclat.* Like all Frenchmen he has a passion for stage effect. Every action that breathes of generosity is poisoned by this calculation. His star, his love of glory, his doctrine of the immortality of the soul, are all French. " I must dazzle and astonish. If I were to give the liberty of the press, my power could not last three days." To make a great noise is his favorite design. " A great reputation is a great noise : the more there is made, the farther off it is heard. Laws, institutions, monuments, nations, all fall ; but the noise continues, and resounds in after ages." His doctrine of immortality is simply fame. His theory of influence is not flattering. " There are two levers for moving men, — interest and fear. Love is a silly infatuation, depend upon it. Friendship is but a name. I love nobody. I do not even love my brothers: perhaps Joseph a little, from habit, and because he is my elder; and Duroc, I love him too; but why? — because his character pleases me: he is stern and resolute, and I believe the fellow never shed a tear. For my part I know very well that I have no true friends. As long as I continue to be what I am, I may have as many pretended friends as I please. Leave sensibility to women; but men should be firm in heart and purpose, or they should have nothing to do with war and government." He was thoroughly unscrupulous. He would steal, slander, assassinate, drown and poison, as his interest dictated. He had no generosity, but mere vulgar hatred; he was intensely selfish; he was perfidious; he cheated at cards; he was a prodigious gossip, and opened letters, and delighted in his infamous police, and rubbed his hands with joy when he had intercepted some morsel of intelligence concerning the men and women about him, boasting that "he knew every thing;" and interfered with the cutting the dresses of the women; and listened after the hurrahs and the compliments of the street, incognito. His manners were coarse. He treated women with low familiarity. He had the habit of pulling their ears

and pinching their cheeks when he was in good
humor, and of pulling the ears and whiskers of
men, and of striking and horse-play with them, to
his last days. It does not appear that he listened
at key-holes, or at least that he was caught at it.
In short, when you have penetrated through all the
circles of power and splendor, you were not deal-
ing with a gentleman, at last; but with an impostor
and a rogue ; and he fully deserves the epithet of
Jupiter Scapin, or a sort of Scamp Jupiter.

In describing the two parties into which modern
society divides itself, — the democrat and the conservative, — I said, Bonaparte represents the Democrat, or the party of men of business, against the
stationary or conservative party. I omitted then
to say, what is material to the statement, namely
that these two parties differ only as young and old.
The democrat is a young conservative ; the conservative is an old democrat. The aristocrat is the
democrat ripe and gone to seed ; — because both
parties stand on the one ground of the supreme
value of property, which one endeavors to get, and
the other to keep. Bonaparte may be said to represent the whole history of this party, its youth and
its age ; yes, and with poetic justice its fate, in his
own. The counter-revolution, the counter-party,
still waits for its organ and representative, in a

lover and a man of truly public and universal aims.

Here was an experiment, under the most favorable conditions, of the powers of intellect without conscience. Never was such a leader so endowed and so weaponed; never leader found such aids and followers. And what was the result of this vast talent and power, of these immense armies, burned cities, squandered treasures, immolated millions of men, of this demoralized Europe? It came to no result. All passed away like the smoke of his artillery, and left no trace. He left France smaller, poorer, feebler, than he found it; and the whole contest for freedom was to be begun again. The attempt was in principle suicidal. France served him with life and limb and estate, as long as it could identify its interest with him; but when men saw that after victory was another war; after the destruction of armies, new conscriptions; and they who had toiled so desperately were never nearer to the reward, — they could not spend what they had earned, nor repose on their down-beds, nor strut in their chateaux, — they deserted him. Men found that his absorbing egotism was deadly to all other men. It resembled the torpedo, which inflicts a succession of shocks on any one who takes hold of it, producing spasms which contract the muscles of the hand, so that the man can not open his fingers;

and the animal inflicts new and more violent shocks, until he paralyzes and kills his victim. So this exorbitant egotist narrowed, impoverished and absorbed the power and existence of those who served him; and the universal cry of France and of Europe in 1814 was, "Enough of him;" "*Assez de Bonaparte.*"

It was not Bonaparte's fault. He did all that in him lay to live and thrive without moral principle. It was the nature of things, the eternal law of man and of the world which baulked and ruined him; and the result, in a million experiments, will be the same. Every experiment, by multitudes or by individuals, that has a sensual and selfish aim, will fail. The pacific Fourier will be as inefficient as the pernicious Napoleon. As long as our civilization is essentially one of property, of fences, of exclusiveness, it will be mocked by delusions. Our riches will leave us sick; there will be bitterness in our laughter, and our wine will burn our mouth. Only that good profits which we can taste with all doors open, and which serves all men.

GOETHE; OR, THE WRITER.

VII.

GOETHE; OR, THE WRITER.

———◆———

I FIND a provision in the constitution of the world for the writer, or secretary, who is to report the doings of the miraculous spirit of life that everywhere throbs and works. His office is a reception of the facts into the mind, and then a selection of the eminent and characteristic experiences.

Nature will be reported. All things are engaged in writing their history. The planet, the pebble, goes attended by its shadow. The rolling rock leaves its scratches on the mountain; the river its channel in the soil; the animal its bones in the stratum; the fern and leaf their modest epitaph in the coal. The falling drop makes its sculpture in the sand or the stone. Not a foot steps into the snow or along the ground, but prints, in characters more or less lasting, a map of its march. Every act of the man inscribes itself in the memories of his fellows and in his own manners and face. The air is full of sounds; the sky, of tokens; the ground is all memoranda and signatures, and every object covered over with hints which speak to the intelligent.

In nature, this self-registration is incessant, and the narrative is the print of the seal. It neither exceeds nor comes short of the fact. But nature strives upward; and, in man, the report is something more than print of the seal. It is a new and finer form of the original. The record is alive, as that which it recorded is alive. In man, the memory is a kind of looking-glass, which, having received the images of surrounding objects, is touched with life, and disposes them in a new order. The facts do not lie in it inert; but some subside and others shine; so that soon we have a new picture, composed of the eminent experiences. The man co-operates. He loves to communicate; and that which is for him to say lies as a load on his heart until it is delivered. But, besides the universal joy of conversation, some men are born with exalted powers for this second creation. Men are born to write. The gardener saves every slip and seed and peach-stone: his vocation is to be a planter of plants. Not less does the writer attend his affair. Whatever he beholds or experiences, comes to him as a model and sits for its picture. He counts it all nonsense that they say, that some things are undescribable. He believes that all that can be thought can be written, first or last; and he would

report the Holy Ghost, or attempt it. Nothing
so broad, so subtle, or so dear, but comes therefore
commended to his pen, and he will write. In his
eyes, a man is the faculty of reporting, and the
universe is the possibility of being reported. In
conversation, in calamity, he finds new materials;
as our German poet said, "Some god gave me the
power to paint what I suffer." He draws his rents
from rage and pain. By acting rashly, he buys the
power of talking wisely. Vexations and a tempest
of passion only fill his sail; as the good Luther
writes, "When I am angry, I can pray well and
preach well:" and, if we knew the genesis of fine
strokes of eloquence, they might recall the complai-
sance of Sultan Amurath, who struck off some
Persian heads, that his physician, Vesalius, might
see the spasms in the muscles of the neck. His
failures are the preparation of his victories. A
new thought or a crisis of passion apprises him
that all that he has yet learned and written is ex-
oteric, — is not the fact, but some rumor of the
fact. What then? Does he throw away the pen?
No; he begins again to describe in the new light
which has shined on him, — if, by some means, he
may yet save some true word. Nature conspires.
Whatever can be thought can be spoken, and still
rises for utterance, though to rude and stammering
organs. If they cannot compass it, it waits and

works, until at last it moulds them to its perfect will and is articulated.

This striving after imitative expression, which one meets every where, is significant of the aim of nature, but is mere stenography. There are higher degrees, and nature has more splendid endowments for those whom she elects to a superior office ; for the class of scholars or writers, who see connection where the multitude see fragments, and who are impelled to exhibit the facts in order, and so to supply the axis on which the frame of things turns. Nature has dearly at heart the formation of the speculative man, or scholar. It is an end never lost sight of, and is prepared in the original casting of things. He is no permissive or accidental appearance, but an organic agent, one of the estates of the realm, provided and prepared from of old and from everlasting, in the knitting and contexture of things. Presentiments, impulses, cheer him. There is a certain heat in the breast which attends the perception of a primary truth, which is the shining of the spiritual sun down into the shaft of the mine. Every thought which dawns on the mind, in the moment of its emergence announces its own rank, — whether it is some whimsy, or whether it is a power.

If he have his incitements, there is, on the other side, invitation and need enough of his gift. Society has, at all times, the same want, namely of one sane man with adequate powers of expression to hold up each object of monomania in its right relations. The ambitious and mercenary bring their last new mumbo-jumbo, whether tariff, Texas, railroad, Romanism, mesmerism, or California; and, by detaching the object from its relations, easily succeed in making it seen in a glare; and a multitude go mad about it, and they are not to be reproved or cured by the opposite multitude who are kept from this particular insanity by an equal frenzy on another crotchet. But let one man have the comprehensive eye that can replace this isolated prodigy in its right neighborhood and bearings, — the illusion vanishes, and the returning reason of the community thanks the reason of the monitor.

The scholar is the man of the ages, but he must also wish with other men to stand well with his contemporaries. But there is a certain ridicule, among superficial people, thrown on the scholars or clerisy, which is of no import unless the scholar heed it. In this country, the emphasis of conversation and of public opinion commends the practical man; and the solid portion of the community is named with significant respect in every circle. Our people are of Bonaparte's opinion concerning ideologists. Ideas are subversive of social order and comfort, and at last make a fool of the possessor.

It is believed, the ordering a cargo of goods from New York to Smyrna, or the running up and down to procure a company of subscribers to set a-going five or ten thousand spindles, or the negotiations of a caucus and the practising on the prejudices and facility of country-people to secure their votes in November, — is practical and commendable.

If I were to compare action of a much higher strain with a life of contemplation, I should not venture to pronounce with much confidence in favor of the former. Mankind have such a deep stake in inward illumination, that there is much to be said by the hermit or monk in defence of his life of thought and prayer. A certain partiality, a headiness and loss of balance, is the tax which all action must pay. Act, if you like, — but you do it at your peril. Men's actions are too strong for them. Show me a man who has acted and who has not been the victim and slave of his action. What they have done commits and enforces them to do the same again. The first act, which was to be an experiment, becomes a sacrament. The fiery reformer embodies his aspiration in some rite or covenant, and he and his friends cleave to the form and lose the aspiration. The Quaker has established Quakerism, the Shaker has established his monastery and his dance; and although each prates of spirit, there is no spirit, but repetition, which is anti-spiritual. But where are his new things of to-day? In actions of enthusiasm this drawback appears, but in those lower activities, which have no higher aim than to make us more comfortable and more cowardly; in actions of cunning, actions that steal and lie, actions that divorce the speculative from the practical faculty and put a ban on reason and sentiment, there is nothing else but drawback and negation. The Hindoos write in their sacred books, "Children only, and not the learned, speak of the speculative and the practical faculties as two. They are but one, for both obtain the selfsame end, and the place which is gained by the followers of the one is gained by the followers of the other. That man seeth, who seeth that the speculative and the practical doctrines are one." For great action must draw on the spiritual nature. The measure of action is the sentiment from which it proceeds. The greatest action may easily be one of the most private circumstance.

This disparagement will not come from the leaders, but from inferior persons. The robust gentlemen who stand at the head of the practical class, share the ideas of the time, and have too much sympathy with the speculative class. It is not from men excellent in any kind that disparagement of any other is to be looked for. With such,

Talleyrand's question is ever the main one; not, is he rich? is he committed? is he well-meaning? has he this or that faculty? is he of the movement? is he of the establishment? — but, *Is he any body?* does he stand for something? He must be good of his kind. That is all that Talleyrand, all that State-street, all that the common-sense of mankind asks. Be real and admirable, not as we know, but as you know. Able men do not care in what kind a man is able, so only that he is able. A master likes a master, and does not stipulate whether it be orator, artist, craftsman, or king.

Society has really no graver interest than the well-being of the literary class. And it is not to be denied that men are cordial in their recognition and welcome of intellectual accomplishments. Still the writer does not stand with us on any commanding ground. I think this to be his own fault. A pound passes for a pound. There have been times when he was a sacred person: he wrote Bibles, the first hymns, the codes, the epics, tragic songs, Sibylline verses, Chaldean oracles, Laconian sentences, inscribed on temple walls. Every word was true, and woke the nations to new life. He wrote without levity and without choice. Every word was carved before his eyes into the earth and the sky; and the sun and stars were only letters of the same purport and of no more necessity. But how can he be honored when he does not honor himself; when he loses himself in the crowd; when he is no longer the lawgiver, but the sycophant, ducking to the giddy opinion of a reckless public; when he must sustain with shameless advocacy some bad government, or must bark, all the year round, in opposition; or write conventional criticism, or profligate novels; or at any rate write without thought, and without recurrence by day and by night to the sources of inspiration?

Some reply to these questions may be furnished by looking over the list of men of literary genius in our age. Among these no more instructive name occurs than that of Goethe to represent the powers and duties of the scholar or writer.

I described Bonaparte as a representative of the popular external life and aims of the nineteenth century. Its other half, its poet, is Goethe, a man quite domesticated in the century, breathing its air, enjoying its fruits, impossible at any earlier time, and taking away, by his colossal parts, the reproach of weakness which but for him would lie on the intellectual works of the period. He appears at a time when a general culture has spread itself and has smoothed down all sharp individual traits; when, in the absence of heroic characters, a social comfort and co-operation have come in. There is no poet, but scores of poetic writers; no Columbus, but hundreds of post-captains, with transit-telescope, barometer and concentrated soup and pemmican ; no Demosthenes, no Chatham, but any number of clever parliamentary and forensic debaters ; no prophet or saint, but colleges of divinity ; no learned man, but learned societies, a cheap press, reading-rooms and book-clubs without number. There was never such a miscellany of facts. The world extends itself like American trade. We conceive Greek or Roman life, life in the Middle Ages, to be a simple and comprehensible affair; but modern life to respect a multitude of things, which is distracting.

Goethe was the philosopher of this multiplicity ; hundred-handed, Argus-eyed, able and happy to cope with this rolling miscellany of facts and sciences, and by his own versatility to dispose of them with ease ; a manly mind, unembarrassed by the variety of coats of convention with which life had got encrusted, easily able by his subtlety to pierce these and to draw his strength from nature, with which he lived in full communion. What is strange too, he lived in a small town, in a petty state, in a defeated state, and in a time when Germany played no such leading part in the world's affairs as to swell the bosom of her sons with any metropolitan pride, such as might have cheered a French, or English, or once, a Roman or Attic

genius. Yet there is no trace of provincial limitation in his muse. He is not a debtor to his position,
but was born with a free and controlling genius.

The Helena, or the second part of Faust, is a
philosophy of literature set in poetry ; the work of
one who found himself the master of histories, mythologies, philosophies, sciences and national literatures, in the encyclopædical manner in which modern erudition, with its international intercourse of
the whole earth's population, researches into Indian, Etruscan and all Cyclopean arts ; geology,
chemistry, astronomy ; and every one of these kingdoms assuming a certain aerial and poetic character, by reason of the multitude. One looks at a
king with reverence ; but if one should chance to
be at a congress of kings, the eye would take liberties with the peculiarities of each. These are not
wild miraculous songs, but elaborate forms to which
the poet has confided the results of eighty years of
observation. This reflective and critical wisdom
makes the poem more truly the flower of this time.
It dates itself. Still he is a poet, — poet of a
prouder laurel than any contemporary, and, under
this plague of microscopes (for he seems to see out
of every pore of his skin), strikes the harp with a
hero's strength and grace.

The wonder of the book is its superior intelligence. In the menstruum of this man's wit, the

past and the present ages, and their religions, politics and modes of thinking, are dissolved into
archetypes and ideas.   What new mythologies sail
through his head !   The Greeks said that Alexander went as far as Chaos; Goethe went, only the
other day, as far ; and one step farther he hazarded,
and brought himself safe back.

There is a heart-cheering freedom in his speculation.   The immense horizon which journeys with
us lends its majesty to trifles and to matters of
convenience and necessity, as to solemn and festal
performances.   He was the soul of his century.   If
that was learned, and had become, by population,
compact organization and drill of parts, one great
Exploring Expedition, accumulating a glut of facts
and fruits too fast for any hitherto-existing *savans*
to classify, — this man's mind had ample chambers
for the distribution of all.   He had a power to
unite the detached atoms again by their own law.
He has clothed our modern existence with poetry.
Amid littleness and detail, he detected the Genius
of life, the old cunning Proteus, nestling close
beside us, and showed that the dulness and prose
we ascribe to the age was only another of his
masks : —

    " His very flight is presence in disguise : "

— that he had put off a gay uniform for a fatigue

dress, and was not a whit less vivacious or rich in Liverpool or the Hague than once in Rome or Antioch. He sought him in public squares and main streets, in boulevards and hotels; and, in the solidest kingdom of routine and the senses, he showed the lurking dæmonic power; that, in actions of routine, a thread of mythology and fable spins itself: and this, by tracing the pedigree of every usage and practice, every institution, utensil and means, home to its origin in the structure of man. He had an extreme impatience of conjecture and of rhetoric. "I have guesses enough of my own; if a man write a book, let him set down only what he knows." He writes in the plainest and lowest tone, omitting a great deal more than he writes, and putting ever a thing for a word. He has explained the distinction between the antique and the modern spirit and art. He has defined art, its scope and laws. He has said the best things about nature that ever were said. He treats nature as the old philosophers, as the seven wise masters did, — and, with whatever loss of French tabulation and dissection, poetry and humanity remain to us; and they have some doctoral skill. Eyes are better on the whole than telescopes or microscopes. He has contributed a key to many parts of nature, through the rare turn for unity and simplicity in his mind. Thus Goethe suggested the leading idea

of modern botany, that a leaf or the eye of a leaf
is the unit of botany, and that every part of the
plant is only a transformed leaf to meet a new condition ; and, by varying the conditions, a leaf may
be converted into any other organ, and any other
organ into a leaf.   In like manner, in osteology, he
assumed that one vertebra of the spine might be
considered as the unit of the skeleton : the head
was only the uppermost vertebræ transformed.
" The plant goes from knot to knot, closing at last
with the flower and the seed.   So the tape-worm,
the caterpillar, goes from knot to knot and closes
with the head.   Man and the higher animals are
built up through the vertebræ, the powers being
concentrated in the head."   In optics again he re-
jected the artificial theory of seven colors, and considered that every color was the mixture of light
and darkness in new proportions.   It is really of
very little consequence what topic he writes upon.
He sees at every pore, and has a certain gravitation towards truth.   He will realize what you say.
He hates to be trifled with and to be made to say
over again some old wife's fable that has had possession of men's faith these thousand years.   He
may as well see if it is true as another.   He sifts
it.   I am here, he would say, to be the measure and
judge of these things.   Why should I take them
on trust ?   And therefore what he says of religion,

of passion, of marriage, of manners, of property, of paper-money, of periods of belief, of omens, of luck, or whatever else, refuses to be forgotten.

Take the most remarkable example that could occur of this tendency to verify every term in popular use. The Devil had played an important part in mythology in all times. Goethe would have no word that does not cover a thing. The same measure will still serve: " I have never heard of any crime which I might not have committed." So he flies at the throat of this imp. He shall be real; he shall be modern; he shall be European; he shall dress like a gentleman, and accept the manners, and walk in the streets, and be well initiated in the life of Vienna and of Heidelberg in 1820, — or he shall not exist. Accordingly, he stripped him of mythologic gear, of horns, cloven foot, harpoon tail, brimstone and blue-fire, and instead of looking in books and pictures, looked for him in his own mind, in every shade of coldness, selfishness and unbelief that, in crowds or in solitude, darkens over the human thought, — and found that the portrait gained reality and terror by every thing he added and by every thing he took away. He found that the essence of this hobgoblin which had hovered in shadow about the habitations of men ever since there were men, was pure intellect, applied, — as always there is a tendency, — to the service of the senses: and he flung into literature, in his Mephistopheles, the first organic figure that has been added for some ages, and which will remain as long as the Prometheus.

I have no design to enter into any analysis of his numerous works. They consist of translations, criticism, dramas, lyric and every other description of poems, literary journals and portraits of distinguished men. Yet I cannot omit to specify the "Wilhelm Meister."

"Wilhelm Meister" is a novel in every sense, the first of its kind, called by its admirers the only delineation of modern society, — as if other novels, those of Scott for example, dealt with costume and condition, this with the spirit of life. It is a book over which some veil is still drawn. It is read by very intelligent persons with wonder and delight. It is preferred by some such to Hamlet, as a work of genius. I suppose no book of this century can compare with it in its delicious sweetness, so new, so provoking to the mind, gratifying it with so many and so solid thoughts, just insights into life and manners and characters; so many good hints for the conduct of life, so many unexpected glimpses into a higher sphere, and never a trace of rhetoric or dulness. A very provoking book to the curiosity of young men of genius, but a very unsatisfactory one. Lovers of light reading, those who look in it for the entertainment they find in a romance, are disappointed. On the other hand, those who begin it with the higher hope to read in it a worthy history of genius, and the just award of the laurel to its toils and denials, have also reason to complain. We had an English romance here, not long ago, professing to embody the hope of a new age and to unfold the political hope of the party called 'Young England,' — in which the only reward of virtue is a seat in Parliament and a peerage. Goethe's romance has a conclusion as lame and immoral. George Sand, in Consuelo and its continuation, has sketched a truer and more dignified picture. In the progress of the story, the characters of the hero and heroine expand at a rate that shivers the porcelain chess-table of aristocratic convention: they quit the society and habits of their rank, they lose their wealth, they become the servants of great ideas and of the most generous social ends; until at last the hero, who is the centre and fountain of an association for the rendering of the noblest benefits to the human race, no longer answers to his own titled name; it sounds foreign and remote in his ear. " I am only man," he says; " I breathe and work for man ; " and this in poverty and extreme sacrifices. Goethe's hero, on the contrary, has so many weak-

nesses and impurities and keeps such bad company, that the sober English public, when the
book was translated, were disgusted. And yet it
is so crammed with wisdom, with knowledge of
the world and with knowledge of laws; the persons so truly and subtly drawn, and with such few
strokes, and not a word too much, — the book remains ever so new and unexhausted, that we must
even let it go its way and be willing to get what
good from it we can, assured that it has only
begun its office and has millions of readers yet to
serve.

The argument is the passage of a democrat to
the aristocracy, using both words in their best
sense. And this passage is not made in any mean
or creeping way, but through the hall door. Nature and character assist, and the rank is made
real by sense and probity in the nobles. No generous youth can escape this charm of reality in
the book, so that it is highly stimulating to intellect and courage.

The ardent and holy Novalis characterized the
book as " thoroughly modern and prosaic; the romantic is completely levelled in it; so is the poetry of nature; the wonderful. The book treats
only of the ordinary affairs of men: it is a poet-
icized civic and domestic story. The wonderful
in it is expressly treated as fiction and enthusi-

astic dreaming:"—and yet, what is also characteristic, Novalis soon returned to this book, and
it remained his favorite reading to the end of his
life.

What distinguishes Goethe for French and
English readers is a property which he shares
with his nation,—a habitual reference to interior
truth. In England and in America there is a
respect for talent; and, if it is exerted in support
of any ascertained or intelligible interest or party,
or in regular opposition to any, the public is satisfied. In France there is even a greater delight
in intellectual brilliancy for its own sake. And
in all these countries, men of talent write from
talent. It is enough if the understanding is occupied, the taste propitiated,—so many columns,
so many hours, filled in a lively and creditable
way. The German intellect wants the French
sprightliness, the fine practical understanding of
the English, and the American adventure; but it
has a certain probity, which never rests in a superficial performance, but asks steadily, *To what
end?* A German public asks for a controlling
sincerity. Here is activity of thought; but what
is it for? What does the man mean? Whence,
whence all these thoughts?

Talent alone can not make a writer. There
must be a man behind the book; a personality

which by birth and quality is pledged to the doctrines there set forth, and which exists to see and
state things so, and not otherwise; holding things
because they are things.   If he cannot rightly
express himself to-day, the same things subsist
and will open themselves to-morrow.   There lies
the burden on his mind, — the burden of truth
to be declared, — more or less understood; and it
constitutes his business and calling in the world
to see those facts through, and to make them
known.   What signifies that he trips and stam-
mers; that his voice is harsh or hissing; that
his method or his tropes are inadequate?   That
message will find method and imagery, articulation
and melody.   Though he were dumb it would
speak.   If not, — if there be no such God's word
in the man, — what care we how adroit, how fluent,
how brilliant he is?

It makes a great difference to the force of any
sentence whether there be a man behind it or no.
In the learned journal, in the influential newspaper, I discern no form; only some irresponsi-
ble shadow ; oftener some moneyed corporation, or
some dangler who hopes, in the mask and robes of
his paragraph, to pass for somebody.   But through
every clause and part of speech of a right book I
meet the eyes of the most determined of men ; his
force and terror inundate every word; the commas

and dashes are alive ; so that the writing is athletic and nimble, — can go far and live long.

In England and America, one may be an adept in the writings of a Greek or Latin poet, without any poetic taste or fire. That a man has spent years on Plato and Proclus, does not afford a presumption that he holds heroic opinions, or undervalues the fashions of his town. But the German nation have the most ridiculous good faith on these subjects : the student, out of the lecture-room, still broods on the lessons ; and the professor can not divest himself of the fancy that the truths of philosophy have some application to Berlin and Munich. This earnestness enables them to outsee men of much more talent. Hence almost all the valuable distinctions which are current in higher conversation have been derived to us from Germany. But whilst men distinguished for wit and learning, in England and France, adopt their study and their side with a certain levity, and are not understood to be very deeply engaged, from grounds of character, to the topic or the part they espouse, — Goethe, the head and body of the German nation, does not speak from talent, but the truth shines through : he is very wise, though his talent often veils his wisdom. However excellent his sentence is, he has somewhat better in view. It awakens my curiosity. He has the formidable independence which converse with truth gives : hear you, or forbear, his fact abides ; and your interest in the writer is not confined to his story and he dismissed from memory when he has performed his task creditably, as a baker when he has left his loaf ; but his work is the least part of him.   The old Eternal Genius who built the world has confided himself more to this man than to any other.

I dare not say that Goethe ascended to the highest grounds from which genius has spoken.   He has not worshipped the highest unity; he is incapable of a self-surrender to the moral sentiment. There are nobler strains in poetry than any he has sounded.   There are writers poorer in talent, whose tone is purer and more touches the heart.   Goethe can never be dear to men.   His is not even the devotion to pure truth ; but to truth for the sake of culture.   He has no aims less large than the conquest of universal nature, of universal truth, to be his portion : a man not to be bribed, nor deceived, nor overawed ; of a stoical self-command and self-denial, and having one test for all men, — *What can you teach me ?*   All possessions are valued by him for that only ; rank, privileges, health, time, Being itself.

He is the type of culture, the amateur of all arts and sciences and events ; artistic, but not artist; spiritual, but not spiritualist.   There is nothing he had not right to know: there is no weapon in the armory of universal genius he did not take into his hand, but with peremptory heed that he should not be for a moment prejudiced by his instruments. He lays a ray of light under every fact, and between himself and his dearest property. From him nothing was hid, nothing withholden. The lurking dæmons sat to him, and the saint who saw the dæmons; and the metaphysical elements took form. "Piety itself is no aim, but only a means whereby through purest inward peace we may attain to highest culture." And his penetration of every secret of the fine arts will make Goethe still more statuesque. His affections help him, like women employed by Cicero to worm out the secret of conspirators. Enmities he has none. Enemy of him you may be, — if so you shall teach him aught which your good-will cannot, were it only what experience will accrue from your ruin. Enemy and welcome, but enemy on high terms. He cannot hate any body; his time is worth too much. Temperamental antagonisms may be suffered, but like feuds of emperors, who fight dignifiedly across kingdoms.

His autobiography, under the title of "Poetry and Truth out of my Life," is the expression of the idea, — now familiar to the world through the German mind, but a novelty to England, Old and

New, when that book appeared, — that a man exists for culture; not for what he can accomplish, but for what can be accomplished in him. The reaction of things on the man is the only noteworthy result. An intellectual man can see himself as a third person; therefore his faults and delusions interest him equally with his successes. Though he wishes to prosper in affairs, he wishes more to know the history and destiny of man; whilst the clouds of egotists drifting about him are only interested in a low success.

This idea reigns in the "Dichtung und Wahrheit" and directs the selection of the incidents; and nowise the external importance of events, the rank of the personages, or the bulk of incomes. Of course the book affords slender materials for what would be reckoned with us a "Life of Goethe;" — few dates, no correspondence, no details of offices or employments, no light on his marriage; and a period of ten years, that should be the most active in his life, after his settlement at Weimar, is sunk in silence. Meantime certain love-affairs that came to nothing, as people say, have the strangest importance: he crowds us with details: — certain whimsical opinions, cosmogonies and religions of his own invention, and especially his relations to remarkable minds and to critical epochs of thought: — these he magnifies. His "Daily and Yearly Journal," his "Italian Travels," his "Campaign in France" and the historical part of his "Theory of Colors," have the same interest. In the last, he rapidly notices Kepler, Roger Bacon, Galileo, Newton, Voltaire, &c.; and the charm of this portion of the book consists in the simplest statement of the relation betwixt these grandees of European scientific history and himself; the mere drawing of the lines from Goethe to Kepler, from Goethe to Bacon, from Goethe to Newton. The drawing of the line is, for the time and person, a solution of the formidable problem, and gives pleasure when Iphigenia and Faust do not, without any cost of invention comparable to that of Iphigenia and Faust.

This lawgiver of art is not an artist. Was it that he knew too much, that his sight was microscopic and interfered with the just perspective, the seeing of the whole? He is fragmentary; a writer of occasional poems and of an encyclopædia of sentences. When he sits down to write a drama or a tale, he collects and sorts his observations from a hundred sides, and combines them into the body as fitly as he can. A great deal refuses to incorporate: this he adds loosely as letters of the parties, leaves from their journals, or the like. A great deal still is left that will not find any place. This the bookbinder alone can give any cohesion to; and hence, notwithstanding the looseness of many of his

works, we have volumes of detached paragraphs,
aphorisms, *Xenien*, &c.

I suppose the worldly tone of his tales grew out
of the calculations of self-culture. It was the in-
firmity of an admirable scholar, who loved the
world out of gratitude; who knew where libraries,
galleries, architecture, laboratories, *savans* and leisure, were to be had, and who did not quite trust
the compensations of poverty and nakedness. Socrates loved Athens; Montaigne, Paris; and Ma-
dame de Staël said she was only vulnerable on that
side (namely, of Paris). It has its favorable as-
pect. All the geniuses are usually so ill-assorted
and sickly that one is ever wishing them somewhere
else. We seldom see any body who is not uneasy
or afraid to live. There is a slight blush of shame
on the cheek of good men and aspiring men, and a
spice of caricature. But this man was entirely at
home and happy in his century and the world.
None was so fit to live, or more heartily enjoyed
the game. In this aim of culture, which is the
genius of his works, is their power. The idea of
absolute, eternal truth, without reference to my
own enlargement by it, is higher. The surrender
to the torrent of poetic inspiration is higher; but
compared with any motives on which books are
written in England and America, this is very truth,
and has the power to inspire which belongs to truth.

Thus has he brought back to a book some of its ancient might and dignity.

Goethe, coming into an over-civilized time and country, when original talent was oppressed under the load of books and mechanical auxiliaries and the distracting variety of claims, taught men how to dispose of this mountainous miscellany and make it subservient. I join Napoleon with him, as being both representatives of the impatience and reaction of nature against the *morgue* of conventions, — two stern realists, who, with their scholars, have severally set the axe at the root of the tree of cant and seeming, for this time and for all time. This cheerful laborer, with no external popularity or provocation, drawing his motive and his plan from his own breast, tasked himself with stints for a giant, and without relaxation or rest, except by alternating his pursuits, worked on for eighty years with the steadiness of his first zeal.

It is the last lesson of modern science that the highest simplicity of structure is produced, not by few elements, but by the highest complexity. Man is the most composite of all creatures; the wheel-insect, *volvox globator*, is at the other extreme. We shall learn to draw rents and revenues from the immense patrimony of the old and the recent ages. Goethe teaches courage, and the equivalence of all times; that the disadvantages of any epoch exist only to the faint-hearted. Genius hovers with his sunshine and music close by the darkest and deafest eras. No mortgage, no attainder, will hold on men or hours. The world is young: the former great men call to us affectionately. We too must write Bibles, to unite again the heavens and the earthly world. The secret of genius is to suffer no fiction to exist for us; to realize all that we know; in the high refinement of modern life, in arts, in sciences, in books, in men, to exact good faith, reality and a purpose; and first, last, midst and without end, to honor every truth by use.

Endicott College Library

PRIDE'S CROSSING, MASS.